A RIGHT TO LIE?

A RIGHT TO LIE?

Presidents, Other Liars, and the First Amendment

Catherine J. Ross

PENN

UNIVERSITY OF PENNSYLVANIA PRESS

PHILADELPHIA

Published by
University of Pennsylvania Press
Philadelphia, Pennsylvania 19104-4112
www.upenn.edu/pennpress

Printed in the United States of America on acid-free paper

10 9 8 7 6 5 4 3 2 1

Library of Congress Cataloging-in-Publication Data

Names: Ross, Catherine J., author.
Title: A right to lie? : presidents, other liars, and the First
Amendment / Catherine J. Ross.
Description: 1st edition. | Philadelphia : University of
Pennsylvania Press, [2021] | Includes bibliographical
references and index.
Identifiers: LCCN 2021019353 | ISBN 9780812253252
(hardcover)
Subjects: LCSH: Freedom of speech—United States. |
United States. Constitution. 1st Amendment. | Truthfulness
and falsehood—Political aspects—United States. |
Deception—Political aspects—United States. | Politicians—
United States—Discipline. | United States—Officials and
employees—Discipline. | United States—Politics and
government—21st century.
Classification: LCC KF4772 .R677 2022 |
DDC 342.7308/53—dc23
LC record available at https://lccn.loc.gov/2021019353

For my son,
Daniel Ross-Rieder—
A truth-seeker

CONTENTS

Every violation of truth is . . . a stab at the heart
of human society.

—Ralph Waldo Emerson

PART I

Truth Matters

CHAPTER 1

Something Is Rotten

I s there any way to stop a president who lies constantly about matters large and small, who regularly displays his disconnection from facts or verifiable reality, and whose lies endanger the nation and threaten the very foundations of democracy? This book approaches that question and more by examining how the First Amendment treats deception in public life.

President Donald J. Trump's mendacity during his term in office and its consequences for the nation highlighted the urgent need to grapple with lies by public officials and in public debate.

But this book is not just about Trump, and it is not just about presidents. As I delve into the First Amendment's treatment of deception I will introduce a range of characters from every walk of public life in situations that implicate factual falsehoods and freedom of expression. They include a minor public official masquerading as a Medal of Honor recipient, purveyors of birtherism, and candidates for office who falsely malign their opponents or even usurp the names of famous people. Their stories, and the outcomes of the resulting court cases, reveal the almost insurmountable constitutional and practical hurdles facing efforts to rein in public deception.

The issues raised by Trump's falsehoods remain salient even after his term has ended. The approximately 80 million voters who chose Joe Biden may have breathed a sigh of relief as their candidate was sworn in, but nearly 74 million others wanted to give Trump a second term. On the eve of Biden's inauguration over two-thirds of Republicans still clung to Trump's biggest lie—that Biden's victory was not legitimate.[1] They either did not perceive that Trump had lied or they did not care.

Social scientists who scrutinized Trump's "use of fabrications, lies, and bullshit" as a "signature feature of his presidency" underscored that Republican

elected officials also appeared not to care. During Trump's first impeachment trial Republican senators first refused to hear any evidence and then,
with one exception, brushed off Congressman Adam Schiff's solemn plea
that "truth matters."[2] But Schiff was right. Truth does matter.

It is one thing to say "truth matters," and quite another to agree about
what is true and what is a lie. To begin with, society would need to define what
statements are not true in the sense that they are verifiably false and agree
about facts (like who won the 2020 election or whether COVID-19 is a "hoax"),
and, finally, choose an arbiter of truth to resolve factual disputes.

The very concept of an arbiter of truth raises the specter of George Orwell's dystopian *1984*, as more than one federal judge has observed. A short
distance separates a government empowered to determine what is true and
what is false from one that—like Oceania in *1984*—limits the very subjects
and language of discourse until the populace is stripped of the ability to
entertain any unorthodox thought. The freedom of speech guaranteed by
the First Amendment expressly aims to protect unorthodox thought—
unpopular views and the ideas of dissidents, which majorities are prone to
label "false." A serious tension exists between protecting free speech under
the First Amendment and combating the spread of falsehoods that can endanger a free society.

A Sampling of Trump's Lies

Donald Trump sets the stage for this book. No other fabricator has the potential Trump had as president to mislead masses of people, and no one
else's lies could cause such serious consequences.

Trump is the poster boy for presidential lies. Big, bold, repeated lies, told
without blinking, were Trump's métier. He was not the first president to dis-
semble or outright lie to the public, and he probably will not be the last. He
was, however, the first president whose deluge of deception rendered the old
joke applicable: "How do you know he's lying? He moves his lips."

This book will not offer a compendium of Trump's brazen mendacity.
Others, such as the *Washington Post*'s fact-checkers and Daniel Dale at
CNN, have counted and catalogued his more than thirty thousand lies during just four years in office.[3] My narrative also sets to the side the actions
that often accompany false statements. Setting conduct aside clarifies the

power of deceptive words and keeps the book's focus on freedom of expression.

Sages, Jesuits, and Talmudic scholars could spend lifetimes debating which is the most significant among Trump's big lies to the public. I focus here on his false claims about his very persona and his baseless attacks on the integrity of the 2020 election. I will address a third, his egregious falsehoods about COVID-19, in Chapter 5.

Who Is Trump?

Trump's 2016 electoral victory built on a foundational lie, the one Trump constructed about his fabricated persona as a brilliant businessman, indeed a billionaire, known to the public as a reality show celebrity who shouted "You're fired" at would-be employees. But Trump is an imposter. He is a vulgar facsimile of the elegant, well-mannered Mr. Ripley—novelist Patricia Highsmith's sociopathic impersonator played by Matt Damon in the film *The Talented Mr. Ripley*.

In the run-up to the 2020 election, the *New York Times* revealed to the public some of what Trump had been so adamant about hiding that he twice fought release of his tax returns all the way to the Supreme Court. Trump had pressed to the limits of creative accounting (and perhaps beyond), paying no federal income taxes at all for ten of the fifteen years before the 2016 election, and a grand total of $750 (that's right, no additional zeroes) in 2016 and again in 2017, his first year in office. It turned out, the *Times* reported, that Trump's side gig on NBC's *The Apprentice* was no hobby; the cash flow it generated apparently saved him from the imminent prospect of seeking a corporate bankruptcy for the fifth or seventh time depending on whether you accept Trump's own count or that of objective journalists.[4]

The *Times* found that Trump, far from being awash in riches, was at least $420 million in debt, loans that he had personally guaranteed and that he would have to pay off in full within a few years. And he was at serious risk of owing the Internal Revenue Service another roughly $100 million pending the outcome of an investigation into whether a refund he had requested and received had been legitimate or would need to be disgorged.

Just weeks later, *Forbes* declared that the *Times* had been too cautious in estimating Trump's debts. Its investigation concluded that Trump was more than $1 billion in debt. Former investment banker William D. Cohan, now a financial writer, asked, "Who knows if he has this kind of money lying around?" Cohan added that his Wall Street contacts "have their serious doubts."[5]

The law posits that voters care about who the candidates really are and that they have a right to find out. It may well be that very few people present a fully accurate public portrait of themselves in everyday life; most probably do not share their fears and blemishes. However, candidates for public office open themselves up for close scrutiny. Lying about the essence of the accomplishments presented as qualifications for office constitutes a betrayal of trust and might be thought to be a major offense.

Trump's posturing was the kind of false presentation that fraudsters engage in to soften up their prey. Sadly, many of Trump's supporters were so locked into the image they held of him that they did not seem to care that he had been revealed as a charlatan.

No federal law requires candidates to present a truthful image of themselves. And even if a statute outlawed Trump's fraudulent autobiographical claims, it would likely prove unconstitutional, as you will see.

The Biggest Lie: Electoral Illegitimacy

That brings us to Trump's most consequential lie: his baseless and unrelenting attacks on the legitimacy of US elections, the fallout from which is still unfolding as this book goes to press. Trump's unsubstantiated challenge to the legitimacy of US elections began even before he assumed office, continued during his presidency, accelerated as it seemed he was likely to lose his 2020 reelection bid, and reached a crescendo after Biden's decisive victory.

Trump had attacked the legitimacy of elections even before he ran for office. In 2012, shortly after Barack Obama won the presidency, Trump (then a private citizen) disputed the election results on Twitter: "We should march on Washington and stop this travesty. . . . This election is a total sham. . . . We are not a democracy!"[6]

During the 2016 campaign, when pollsters and pundits widely expected Trump to lose to Hillary Clinton, he demurred when asked if he would accept the results of the election. His signals were so disturbing that the Obama administration secretly made contingency plans in case Trump's recalcitrance precipitated a constitutional crisis.[7] Trump's surprising Electoral

College victory silenced his challenge to the outcome, but he continued to insist that fraud had cost him a victory in the popular vote.

Between 2012 and early 2020, Trump attacked the legitimacy of our electoral system more than seven hundred times, according to election law expert Richard Hasen. By 2020, facing an uphill battle for reelection, President Trump repeatedly and without any factual basis excoriated the system as "rigged." He increasingly focused his attacks on what he referred to as "mail-in" ballots, which use the same process as the widely accepted "absentee ballots" long available in every jurisdiction, and which Trump and his wife themselves used to vote in Florida's 2020 Republican primary.[8]

He assailed the integrity of the electoral system ninety more times in the first eight months of 2020. In May, for example, he raged on Twitter, "There is NO WAY (ZERO!) that Mail-In Ballots will be anything less than substantially fraudulent." On June 22, Trump tweeted, "RIGGED 2020 ELECTION: MILLIONS OF MAIL-IN BALLOTS WILL BE PRINTED BY FOREIGN COUNTRIES, AND OTHERS. IT WILL BE THE SCANDAL OF OUR TIMES!" In July, he tweeted that 2020 will be "the most RIGGED Election" ever.[9] And on and on.

Trump suggested that the chaos around voting—that he himself had generated—might prevent us from ever knowing who had won: "The Nov 3rd Election result may NEVER BE ACCURATELY DETERMINED."[10] And he informed Fox News interviewer Maria Bartiromo that a do-over might be needed, oblivious to the distinctions between national elections and golf, where an occasional mulligan is permitted.

Trump's advance efforts to delegitimize the election prepared his supporters to repudiate his loss. A Yahoo/YouGov poll in mid-September revealed that only 22 percent of registered voters expected the 2020 election would be "free and fair." Other polls showed that 58 percent to 61 percent of Trump voters anticipated that the only way he was "going to lose in November is if the election is rigged."[11]

Trump's predictions and his insistence after the election that pervasive fraud had occurred flew in the face of studies that showed negligible electoral fraud in the modern United States. Findings by the conservative Heritage Foundation conformed with those of the progressive Brennan Center for Justice and the *Washington Post*, which calculated the level of electoral fraud in recent years at well under a fraction of 1 percent (the highest estimate was 0.002 percent) of all votes cast. That would not be enough to change the outcome in any contest except perhaps the closest and smallest local election.[12]

As Election Day 2020 grew nearer, Trump relied on his own lies about election fraud to double down on his refusal to commit to a peaceful transition of power should he lose. Having already declared that any election he lost would have to be "rigged," Trump insisted that he would have to see if the election was "fair" before conceding.

Trump's false assertions had an impact. In late November, after he lost, 77 percent of Republican voters told Monmouth University pollsters they believed fraud accounted for Biden's victory. At about the same time, 67 percent of those who strongly supported Trump reported to another polling group that they did not believe Biden was the rightful winner, while only 9 percent of that group regarded Biden as the "true winner."[13]

Trump had further undermined confidence in electoral integrity shortly before the election when he swiftly nominated Amy Coney Barrett to the Supreme Court to replace the recently deceased Justice Ruth Bader Ginsburg, whose funeral had not yet taken place. Trump appeared confident that the conservative justices on the court would have his back in any election dispute. That view may have rested in part on the fact that Barrett as well as Justice Brett Kavanaugh (whom he had appointed) and Chief Justice John Roberts had worked for George W. Bush's controversial effort to stop the Florida recount in 2000, which succeeded in giving Bush the presidency.

Instead of lying about the reasons for his unseemly rush to appoint Ginsburg's successor, Trump indulged in one of his periodic bursts of what I call an "explosive truth." He explained that he needed another justice on the court to avoid a four-to-four tie in case it fell to the court to determine the outcome of a close election.

Trump's hopes that millions of votes might be thrown out were dashed when the court rebuffed several meritless claims brought on his behalf. These included a petition to discard the election results in four states initiated by the Republican attorney general of Texas, cosigned by sixteen other attorneys general, and supported by 126 Republican members of the House of Representatives. The court dismissed the case in December without even allowing the petitioners to file briefs.[14] Later, after President Biden took office, Trump chastised the Supreme Court for failing to "overturn" the election.

Trump's lies culminated in an armed insurrection on January 6, 2021—a siege on the Capitol—by Trump's die-hard supporters who believed his unsubstantiated claims that he had won by a landslide. Five people died and over one hundred suffered serious injuries. During the rampage, members of Congress and staff cowered behind barricaded doors. They emerged to a trashed complex.

That episode led a bipartisan majority of the House of Representatives to impeach Trump for an unprecedented second time on the single count of "Incitement of Insurrection." The incitement charge rested on his speech at noon on January 6 to a crowd of supporters gathered on the Ellipse just before Congress was scheduled to take up the final election certification process at 1 P.M. According to the House impeachment charge, Trump "reiterated false claims that 'we won this election, and we won it by a landslide,'" while the mob shouted "FIGHT FOR TRUMP!" Then, he flirted with truth by exhorting them: "We're going to walk down [to the Capitol] and I'll be there with you." Many of those in attendance did walk to the Capitol immediately after Trump's rally ended, and stormed it. Trump, however, did not join them as he had assured them he would.[15]

Trump largely remained silent as the riot proceeded, and when he finally called for the mob to go home he delivered a mixed message by reminding them that the election had been stolen. As the insurrection wound down, and the Capitol was clearing, Trump reached out to claim "a sacred landslide election victory" has been "stripped away from great patriots." In a tweet that was subsequently scrubbed, he insisted that the states needed an opportunity to certify "a corrected set of facts, not the fraudulent or inaccurate ones" scheduled for review in Congress that day: "USA demands the truth!"[16]

Whether one calls the events of January 6 an insurrection, an attempted coup, or something else, Trump's multitude of falsehoods designed to undermine faith in elections stoked the explosion.

The Stakes for Democracy

Those presidential lies endangered the United States. Democracies do not long survive without faith in trustworthy elections followed by the peaceful transfer of power that had long been a hallmark of our constitutional system. Trump attacked the legitimacy of elections and refused to acknowledge his loss while blocking preparations to transfer power. He contaminated the leaders of his party, most of whom declined to rebut his falsehoods and, in many cases, promoted them.

The systemic impact was quick and deep. According to political scientists, Trump's attacks on democratic norms led his followers to "los[e] confidence in elections." Weeks after the election, a sizable number of Republican voters reported they still expected Trump to be sworn in for a second term—even if some may have been posturing for public consumption.[17]

Many Republican members of Congress played into and helped spread Trump's delusional falsehoods. They refused to recognize Biden's victory even after the federal official charged with election security had been fired for asserting that the 2020 election had been the most secure in history, and after Attorney General William Barr had declared that his department had not found any significant evidence of electoral irregularities. In December, when the *Washington Post* asked the 249 Republicans in Congress, "Who won the election?," only twenty-seven acknowledged Biden as the president-elect. Nearly 90 percent declined to answer.[18]

Intransigence by Republican members of Congress endured up to and even after the armed insurrection at the Capitol on January 6 threatened their lives. On the evening of January 6, with order restored to the Capitol, 12 percent of all Republican senators and 57 percent of all Republicans in the House of Representatives voted against certifying the results before Vice President Mike Pence declared Biden the winner. Defying logic, the objectors claimed that their end run around normal procedures would restore integrity and faith in democracy.

Ominously, Trump's big, repeated lie, echoed by his allies, had raised the specter of violence well before January 6. As states certified that Biden had won, numerous reports flowed into the FBI of threats to election officials in states Trump claimed had been stolen.

In Georgia, Republican Gabriel Sterling, a high-ranking election official, was so exasperated he went public with accounts of death threats to rank-and-file election workers: "*It has to stop!*" Addressing President Trump directly, he continued, "Stop inspiring people to commit potential acts of violence. Someone's going to get hurt. Someone's going to get shot. Someone's going to get killed."[19] Within days, dozens of protesters, many heavily armed, converged on the home of Michigan's secretary of state, shouting the pro-Trump slogan "Stop the Steal" while she was decorating the house for Christmas with her four-year-old child.

The disproportionate impact of Trump's lies was underscored after major social media sites banned him in the wake of the January 6 uprising. The digital analytics firm Zignal Labs reported a 73 percent decline in references to election fraud in the week following the ban. Research supported the view that a handful of accounts—including the president's—were "superspreaders" of disinformation.[20]

Although many political leaders and pundits from across the political spectrum declared that democracy had prevailed after Biden assumed office, grave concern remains justified. More than a handful of Republican elected officials still refused to acknowledge that Biden won a fair election after he took the oath of office; they were only willing to admit that he "is the president." Persistent popular belief in unsubstantiated charges about electoral illegitimacy, from assertions of dead people voting, to "fixed" voting machines and more, raises questions about whether and how the United States can return to traditional democratic norms.

Trump mirrored the methods of demagogues the world over. His cornucopia of lies came at such a pace with nearly every news cycle that many people could not fully process or remember them. He embodies the approach widely attributed to Joseph Goebbels, Adolf Hitler's minister of propaganda: "If you tell a lie big enough and keep repeating it, people will eventually come to believe it."[21]

"The decay of truth and democratic dissolution proceed hand in hand," warns historian Ruth Ben-Ghiat, who groups Trump with tyrants from Adolf Hitler and Benito Mussolini to Idi Amin and Saddam Hussein and strongmen today including Viktor Orbán and Vladimir Putin. The strongman's assault on truth begins, she writes, with the "assertion that the establishment media delivers false or biased information while he speaks the truth" and promotes "'real facts.'" Such attacks are easily found in Trump's references to the press as enemies of the people and his harangues about "fake news." His senior counselor Kellyanne Conway's memorable reliance on "alternative facts" encapsulated Trump's assault on truth.[22]

Leading political scientists, like historians, link a blurred distinction between truth and falsehood to the withering away of democratic norms. "President Trump's routine, brazen fabrications are unprecedented" in the United States, according to Steven Levitsky and Daniel Ziblatt, Harvard professors and authors of How Democracies Die. Such mendacity, they write, is dangerous: "Without credible information," citizens "cannot effectively exercise our right to vote." Disinformation, they argue, accelerates the striving authoritarian's ability to pull off four steps toward dismantling democratic structures: rejecting "the democratic rules of the game"; denying the "legitimacy of opponents"; "tolerating or encouraging violence"; and curtailing civil liberties, including attacks on the media.[23]

Yale historian Timothy Snyder, the author of the best seller *On Tyranny: Twenty Lessons from the Twentieth Century*, sums up common methods would-be demagogues rely on to excise reality-based thinking so that they can consolidate power. All of the methods appear in Trump's repertoire: "open hostility to verifiable reality"; "endless repetition"; "magical thinking," which requires "a blatant abandonment of reason"; and "misplaced faith" in a charismatic leader instead of in factual evidence.[24]

A would-be strongman does not necessarily have to ensnare a vast majority of people into his fantasy world. It may be enough to divide the population into warring constituencies.

The ominous splintering of the public into epistemic tribes, each contained in a separate information silo, makes it easy for each side to delegitimize its opponents. A fractured, un-curated stream of information, disinformation, and conspiracy theories online and offline exacerbates the dilemma. People who cannot agree about facts are unlikely to agree about what constitutes a lie or about how to respond to mendacity. The United States faces the risk that each group will continue to demonize the other, deepening the fractures that threaten democracy itself.

Lying to the Public

Given the damage that rampant factual falsehoods can cause, one might reasonably ask why we permit them to flourish. As this book will show, the short answer is that the First Amendment poses nearly insuperable obstacles to regulating deception.

If free and fair voting is the heart of our Republic, the free exchange of ideas is its life blood. The founders committed to robust debate because they viewed freedom of thought and expression as essential to liberty. To protect the circulation of even the least popular ideas, the Speech Clause of the First Amendment provides that "Congress shall make no law . . . abridging the freedom of speech."

"No law," however, is a bit of an overstatement, even among the most ardent advocates for a robust reading of free speech, among whom I count myself. A number of exceptions exist, some of which reach deception.

A range of statutes and legal traditions prohibits carefully defined false statements without offending the Constitution. The deception subject to regulation falls roughly into two sets. The first includes deception that interferes with the administration of justice or the government's functions. For example, it is a crime to commit perjury, lie to government officials under certain circumstances even when not under oath, or make false claims about potential terrorist attacks. The second set generally aims at lies that are likely to materially harm others, particularly people with less access to accurate information than is available to the liar. Examples include fraud, false advertising, and misappropriation of trademarks that confuses consumers. In addition, the First Amendment does not protect certain categories of speech, including defamation (which involves falsehood) and incitement.

The precise constitutional limits to regulation of falsehoods remain unclear, as the articles of impeachment drafted against President Richard M. Nixon illustrate. When Nixon resigned abruptly in 1974 under the threat of imminent impeachment, the charges against him included "making false or misleading public statements for the purpose of deceiving the people." Because Nixon resigned, the impeachment proceedings did not go beyond the preliminary stage. From that point until Trump's second impeachment trial in 2021, Congress never had another occasion to consider whether a president might have a First Amendment right to lie to the public. It made no effort to resolve the question even then.

Later in this book I will explore when and why presidential lies, without more, might amount to an impeachable high crime or misdemeanor. (I leave aside for the moment the question of whether impeachment, conviction, and removal from office remain a practical means of constraining a president.) I will argue that despite the nearly insuperable obstacles that the First Amendment generally poses to regulation of falsehood, the Speech Clause itself offers a doctrinal rationale for constraining significant presidential lies. In the last chapter of this book I will propose a novel approach drawn from an obscure corner of First Amendment jurisprudence: the public employee speech doctrine. Under that analysis, I argue, presidents should have less right to lie than the rest of us because all public employees surrender some of their speech rights as a condition of employment and also because the unique amplification of a president's falsehoods has unparalleled power to harm.

My solution may seem more than a bit quixotic. But it clarifies that the lack of political will presents a more intransigent problem than the First Amendment when it comes to lying presidents.

Defining Lies

Any serious discussion of lies must begin by clarifying how the speaker defines them. Deceptive statements take many rhetorical forms, some of which are indirect or plausibly deniable for other reasons. The method of presentation may make it difficult to establish intent or impose accountability, much less to agree on whether a given statement amounts to a lie.

Sissela Bok, a moral philosopher and the author of the classic *Lying: Moral Choice in Public and Private Life*, has voiced skepticism about counting lies as the widest range of deception. She notes that some commentators on lying include "the shady regions of half-truths, self-deception and hypocrisy" and even unvoiced falsehoods such as those conveyed by a "facial expression or silence."

Bok herself defines a lie more concretely as "any intentionally deceptive message which is stated." She focuses on "clear-cut lies—lies where the intention to mislead is obvious, where the liar knows that what he is communicating is not what he believes, and where he has not deluded himself into believing his own deceits."[25]

I will stick to the legal definitions of the term "lie," though we will also encounter numerous other forms of deception hidden in opinions, innuendo, prevarications, and the like. In law, as in Bok's formulation, a lie requires an intent to deceive, which in turn requires knowledge that a statement is false.

I label the most blatant lies—involving a clear assertion of a verifiable factual falsehood—"bald-faced" (the Supreme Court less colloquially called them "straight-out" lies). Intentional factual falsehoods that can be disproven cannot reasonably be explained away as anything other than lies.

I have crafted a narrower definition for presidential lies than for bald-faced lies. Presidential lies as I use the term do not include every misleading word or misstatement uttered by presidents or on their behalf. The presidential lies that I will argue demand scrutiny are limited to a pattern of verifiable factual falsehoods that materially harm the nation or injure the people of the United States.

But we cannot understand the unique status of presidential deception unless we first analyze the treatment of commonplace lies in the First Amendment's broader scheme.

The next two chapters make up Part II, "No Harm, No Foul." In them, I analyze the gauntlet of legal impediments the First Amendment places in the way of regulating lies that have not demonstrably harmed anyone. Chapter 2 tells the story of Xavier Alvarez, a habitual liar whose false claims to fame landed in the Supreme Court. In 2012, *United States* v. *Alvarez* provided the vehicle for the court's initial declaration that the First Amendment protects lies and liars.

Chapter 3 turns to the Obama-era birtherism controversy, in which Trump and his allies played a critical role, to explicate why it is so difficult to prevail in a defamation case despite the unassailable right of the state to regulate defamatory falsehoods.

Part III, "Lies Affecting Democracy," tackles lies firmly in the political arena. I consider falsehoods in political campaigns before turning to presidential lies. Chapter 4 explains the constitutional and definitional obstacles to regulating lies in political campaigns, focusing on a controversy that culminated in the modern equivalent of an Old West gunfight among the justices of Wisconsin's highest court, torn apart by differences over what counts as a lie in an era of hyper-partisanship.

Chapter 5 uses Trump's repeated lies and denials about COVID-19 to demonstrate the profound harm presidential lies can cause. The lies alone contributed to an accumulation of deaths, long-term ailments, and economic devastation. That carnage, I argue, more than satisfied the Supreme Court's proposition that the Speech Clause might leave room for the state to punish factual falsehoods that cause sufficient harm.

In Chapter 6, I propose that we treat presidents as the public employees they are. Doing so would allow Congress to hold presidents accountable for material verifiable factual falsehoods. Finally, in Chapter 7, after analyzing the role of presidential lies in prior impeachments, I offer a series of steps Congress could take to formalize the norms to which presidents should be held and the actions it could take to enforce those norms before refuting the First Amendment defense offered in President Trump's second impeachment trial in 2021. Throughout, I acknowledge the practical and political hurdles to congressional action in the current climate.

PART II

No Harm, No Foul

CHAPTER 2

Surprise, Lies Are Protected Speech:
United States v. *Alvarez*

On July 23, 2007, Xavier Alvarez, who had recently been elected to represent Pomona, California, on the Three Valleys Municipal Water Board, introduced himself at his first board meeting: "I'm a retired Marine of 25 years. I retired in the year 2001. Back in 1987, I was awarded the Congressional Medal of Honor. I got wounded many times by the same guy. I'm still around." "I'm still around" was the only truthful thing Alvarez said.

Alvarez was a compulsive liar. His own lawyers introduced him to the United States Supreme Court through some of his whoppers: "He lied when he claimed to have played professional hockey for the Detroit Red Wings. He lied when he claimed to be married to a Mexican starlet.... He lied when he claimed to be an engineer. He lied when he claimed to have rescued the American Ambassador during the Iranian hostage crisis, and when he said that he was shot going back to grab the American flag." In Justice Anthony Kennedy's generous view, Alvarez's fabrications amounted to a "pathetic attempt to gain respect that eluded him."[1]

Less gently, to know him was to doubt him. Observers concluded that Alvarez lived in a "make-believe world" and made up stories as a matter of course.[2] Lies seemed to come to him more readily than truth. He lied even when lying did not advantage him in any way. It is easy to imagine his list of lies being set to music, with countless verses and choruses, "he liiied," set to the tune of "She Cried," the 1962 hit by Jay & the Americans.

Unfortunately for Alvarez, he made a fateful miscalculation. Unlike all the other lies he had told in his life, claiming to hold the Congressional

Medal of Honor violated a federal law enacted just two years earlier. Alvarez became one of the first people the federal government prosecuted under the Stolen Valor Act of 2005. That law targeted any person who "falsely represents himself or herself to have been awarded any decoration or medal authorized by Congress for the Armed Forces of the United States" by criminalizing their fabrications.[3] Violations were punishable by fines and up to six months in prison. The act imposed harsher penalties for those who falsely claimed to have received certain awards at the pinnacle of military honors, including the Medal of Honor; those imposters faced a prison term of up to one year, just one day short of a felony offense.

The annals of First Amendment jurisprudence are replete with unsympathetic, disagreeable, and even vicious litigants whose free speech claims prevailed. Many of them seem even less attractive than Alvarez: cross-burners and other racists including Nazis, anti-abortion activists, flag-burners, noxious demonstrators at military funerals, creators of animal snuff films, and misogynists who direct graphically violent lyrics and images at their ex-wives that fall just short of a legal line. That is no accident, because the Speech Clause is designed to protect the dissident, the unpopular, and the cantankerous speaker.

There was no denying that Alvarez lied—even Alvarez spoke truth about his crime. He admitted that he had posed as a Medal of Honor recipient knowing that his claim was not true and that he had wanted others to believe him. He pleaded guilty to violating the Stolen Valor Act while preserving his right to challenge the statute's constitutionality on First Amendment grounds.

Alvarez's challenge to the constitutionality of the Stolen Valor Act's constraint of speech reached the Supreme Court in *United States* v. *Alvarez*, decided in 2012. Before *Alvarez*, the court had never expressly confronted the question of whether intentional lies about verifiable facts had any protection under the Speech Clause. The court seized the occasion to announce that falsehood alone did not strip speech of First Amendment protections. *Alvarez* is the starting point for analyzing the constitutional status of lies.

This chapter analyzes *Alvarez* and its significance. I begin by reviewing the chaotic legal landscape governing the constitutional status of lies before the Supreme Court decided *Alvarez*. The chapter then explores the potential social utility of lies, a subject that several of the appellate judges and Supreme Court justices who ruled on *Alvarez* delved into. Based on that discussion, I take a closer look at Xavier Alvarez the man, and the facts that led to his indictment and guilty plea. Finally, I assess the government's interest in controlling lies about prestigious military awards, before turning to the Supreme Court's resolution of the case and the questions the opinions left unresolved.

The Chaotic Legal Status of Lies Before *Alvarez*

Before 2012, doctrinal chaos surrounded the constitutional status of knowing factual falsehoods. Over the years, the justices had offered various passing comments about falsehood in what lawyers call obiter dicta. Obiter dicta (literally, "by the way") also known as dicta, are observations in a judicial opinion that were not necessary to the outcome of the case, and therefore do not establish reliable precedents for later decisions. And yet lawyers often cite them as indicators of what the law is, or should be. In the lead-up to *Alvarez*, lower courts and scholars offered conflicting interpretations of the Supreme Court's dicta on falsehood. They failed to achieve consensus, though the weight of authority seemed to tilt toward lesser protection for falsehood.

Congress, the Department of Justice, and others can arguably be forgiven their confusion over whether the Speech Clause permitted penalties for simple knowing deceit without any criminal intent or result. So widespread was the belief that deceptive speech lacked First Amendment protection that more than one hundred federal statutes punished intentional falsehoods when *Alvarez* reached the Supreme Court. Federal courts presume that Congress intends its actions to comport with constitutional requirements. Even so, the lack of clarity about the constitutional status of falsity left the distinguished jurists who ruled on *Alvarez* strongly divided as it wended its way through the federal courts.

Although many believed that the Speech Clause did not protect deceptive speech, that conclusion ignored the principle in First Amendment jurisprudence that government regulations on expression based on its content (as opposed to where it is shared or how loudly) is presumptively unconstitutional. A law inhibiting speech is on even shakier constitutional ground if it is based on the speaker's point of view about the content. To identify a lie or any form of misrepresentation, we must scrutinize its content and also conclude that its viewpoint is, at a minimum, incorrect, and often recklessly so.

The Stolen Valor Act was undeniably a content-based regulation. It criminalized a particular intentional falsehood with no additional conditions beyond the expression itself. If deceptions were protected speech, the statute would be presumptively unconstitutional. The court would apply strict scrutiny, the standard courts impose in cases involving fundamental rights, including the First Amendment right to free speech, and could be expected to overturn the law. If, however, all lies, or this kind of bald-faced lie about military service, fell outside the First Amendment's protection, the government would prevail.

When Xavier Alvarez appealed his conviction on First Amendment grounds, two of the three judges on the Ninth Circuit panel agreed with him. They overturned the act and found that the government had unlawfully applied it to Alvarez. The panel first rejected the government's argument that false statements of fact have no constitutional protection unless in any "particular case" the speaker shows that the falsehood deserves First Amendment protection. The government's formulation would have forced the person accused of violating the act to prove that his speech was protected, a stunning reversal of First Amendment principles. The First Amendment requires the government to show why it should be allowed to regulate the speech it has infringed upon by proving that it meets all three elements of strict scrutiny: the government has a compelling governmental interest; the regulation is necessary to achieve that interest; and the regulation is narrowly tailored so that it does not reach more expression than is required to achieve the compelling interest.

The Ninth Circuit panel ruled that factual falsehoods do not fall within any recognized "categorical exception" to the First Amendment. Categorical exceptions refer to categories of expression that have historically been excluded from protection under the Speech Clause based on their potential for harm or the conclusion that they add little if anything to discourse. The categories include incitement to imminent violence, obscenity and child pornography, speech integral to criminal conduct, true threats and what are known as fighting words, fraud, and defamation. Only defamation involves untruthful expression, but it has nothing to do with Alvarez's case. He made false claims about himself, not about a third party, and the falsehoods were intended to boost his reputation, not damage it.

Since no categorical exception covered lies in general, the panel held, falsehoods are protected speech, and strict scrutiny applied. The court held that the statute did not survive strict scrutiny and was unconstitutionally applied to Alvarez, who "was proven to be nothing more than a liar, without more."[4]

The Department of Justice took the rare step of seeking an opportunity to argue the case again before either the same panel or the full Ninth Circuit Court of Appeals through en banc review. En banc review, an unusual procedure reserved for doctrinally significant cases, involves review by all of the judges in the federal appellate circuit sitting together. A majority of the Ninth Circuit judges denied both requests, leaving the panel decision that overturned the Stolen Valor Act in place. However, the case raised sufficiently important issues that individual judges on the full appellate court wrote dueling opinions explaining, on the one hand, why the panel decision overturning the act was correct and, on the other, arguing that en banc review was warranted because the act should be upheld.

Defending the statute and its application to Xavier Alvarez, the Department of Justice stridently argued that intentional lies had no First Amendment value at all. It advanced the novel view that false statements should be added to the short list of categorical exceptions to the Speech Clause, joining fraud, defamation, obscenity, and other exclusions.

Alvarez presented two primary legal questions to the Supreme Court. First, were lies categorically excluded from First Amendment protection, as the government asserted? Second, if the First Amendment protects lies, what standard of review applies, and would the Stolen Valor Act survive that review?

The Social and Political Utility of Lies

Before turning to those constitutional questions that touch on whether falsehood can promote First Amendment values, let us consider whether lies have any value in social life and discourse. *United States* v. *Alvarez* offered a platform for a broader discussion of the social function of lies that was not confined to classical legal analysis. The political philosophy, social science, and prosaic aspects of deception all received attention at oral arguments in the Supreme Court, in Justice Stephen Breyer's concurring opinion, and in an opinion on the denial of appellate review by Chief Judge Alex Kozinski in the Ninth Circuit Court of Appeals.

A hypothetical known as the Nazi at the door is often used to test the morality of and justifications for lying. In this problem, a person opens her front door to Nazi officers seeking hidden Jews. May the person who opens the door lie to protect the Jews in her cellar? If it were illegal to lie as a general matter, and always immoral to lie, she would have to confess that she was sheltering Jews; her guests would be deported or shot on the spot, and she herself would be arrested. This is the stuff of many wonderful films set in World War II Europe. The audience holds its collective breath waiting to see if the host will heroically lie and get away with it.

I think this is a lie a courageous person should tell. I hope if I were ever in that position I would find the strength to carry through. One might even argue that if the host would so easily betray the Jews she had promised to protect she was lying to herself about her heroism all along. And bravery might be reinforced by the knowledge that the Nazis would not be inclined to forgive and forget if the host gives her guests away.

Professional moral philosophers, however, probe the reasoning. Absolute moralists would rule out lying even to save lives. According to Saint Augustine, even a well-intentioned lie deprives the liar of eternal life. Other philosophers inquire into the motivation for lying as they debate whether saving a life justifies violating the Ten Commandments.[5]

The Nazi searching for Jews in the cellar is a subset of a problem traceable to biblical times: the murderer at the door. This oft-discussed hypothetical begins with a would-be murderer chasing his victim to the front door of your home. He asks you "whether our friend has taken refuge in your house." The problem assumes you are hiding the potential victim and asks whether you should tell the truth or lie. This is perhaps the easiest setting for saying a lie is preferred. Lying would save a presumably innocent life, and it appears that the potential victim is your friend. Even if the victim were a stranger, the influential moralist Samuel Johnson said you may always lie "if a murderer should ask you which way a man has gone."[6]

Some commentators impose additional conditions. They argue that one should first ascertain whether the murderer can be dissuaded. Perhaps, some add, one should try to physically restrain the prospective murderer. Others conclude that lies are morally justified whenever innocent lives are in jeopardy. Does this mean you must first ascertain why the murderer seeks to kill the person who is fleeing and whether the person in peril is actually innocent? In these extraordinary circumstances we assume there is not enough time to sort out such details.

Regardless, as a matter of social policy we should discourage the murder because it would be an extralegal means of dispute settlement. Whatever the potential victim might have done, civilized societies governed by rule of law give exclusive control of justice and violence to the state.

When the Supreme Court heard oral argument in *Alvarez*, several justices pursued the Nazis at the door variation of this morality play in order to probe whether bald-faced lies could ever have First Amendment value. After Alvarez's court-appointed attorney asserted that personal autonomy protects lies that do not harm another person or impinge on a government function, Justice Breyer interjected, "Are there Jews hiding in the cellar? No." Breyer's example accounts for the harm that would follow if the Jews' hiding place were revealed, justifying the lie "no," but overlooks the fact that the Nazis at the door were in fact the government; lying would impinge on a government function. The issue becomes more complicated than Alvarez's attorney envisioned—individuals need to assess the government's claim to obedience.

In the United States, lying to government investigators is a felony because it interferes with fact-finding, justice, and governmental efficiency. This proposition raises questions about collaboration and resistance. Lying to government investigators about sheltering an undocumented two-year-old immigrant who would be sent to detention in Texas if ICE discovered her is a crime. Depending on one's political and moral values, lying to protect that toddler might look a lot like lying to the Nazis about Jews in the cellar: a noble, though criminal, act.

In the Supreme Court even Justice Breyer's less complex example needed unraveling. Chief Justice John Roberts responded that the example Breyer offered was not strictly analogous to the facts about Xavier Alvarez. The question "Are there Jews?" did not require an answer based on "a statement about oneself" like Alvarez's lie about receiving the Medal. Breyer refined his hypothetical: "Are *you* hiding Jews in the cellar?" Roberts sought to further differentiate between the person hiding Jews and Alvarez. Justice Breyer's hypothetical, the Chief Justice chided, was not a person "simply telling a false statement about himself. It is about whether there is someone hiding in the attic." The audience laughed.

The Stolen Valor Act reaches "just a purely false statement about one's self," the Chief Justice said. It has, he continued, no exception "to avoid the discovery of someone who should be hidden," which, he implied, might serve First Amendment values. He did not specify which ones, but he may have meant political activism, personal autonomy (acting on one's deepest convictions), or both.

Sociobiologists have argued that lying serves evolutionary purposes. Being less than forthright can help form and sustain relationships, including alliances between tribes, families, and countries; it can smooth business and social dealings and contain family strife.

An everyday example involves Bob's invitation, "Let's have lunch." Alice, eager for that lunch, whips out her phone to schedule, but Carol, who finds the invitation less alluring, has constricted options under common formulations of polite behavior. The script tells Carol to prevaricate, "I'd love to. I'll give you a call to schedule." Of course, one never knows if Bob really wanted to have lunch with either of them. Perhaps he was just trying to extricate himself from the current conversation. These conventions underpin the joke, "When would be a good day for lunch?" "Never." Saying "never," tempting as it might be, violates every norm.

Saying let's have lunch when one does not mean it, or politely dodging that invitation, is a particular form of prevarication that is quite distinct from the factual lie that Alvarez told in claiming the Medal of Honor. If we step back from the strictures of the Stolen Valor Act and think in more ordinary terms, it is unclear exactly what kind of lie Alvarez told. His false claim did not appear to serve any instrumental purpose. Some might call his words "humbug," "bullshit," or barstool braggadocio rather than an outright lie.[7] Alvarez did not anticipate any measurable award for being an imposter, except to look more impressive to others. Because he had already won election to the Water Board, he could not have been hoping for an electoral advantage. There was no prospect of a monetary gain or of using his enhanced reputation to someone else's detriment.

Even "false factual statements," Justice Breyer wrote, concurring in *Alvarez*, "can serve useful human objectives." He pointed to prosaic uses of falsehoods in several settings. In "social contexts" lies may prevent embarrassment, protect privacy, comfort the sick or dying, or preserve a child's belief in the tooth fairy. In "public contexts," lies may reassure a panicking public. And in disputes over ideas, lies may promote reasoning that helps us "realize the truth," as when used to play devil's advocate or in the Socratic method where the intentional lie that serves a pedagogical purpose is often presented as a genuine argument, not as a teaching device.[8]

Justice Breyer's brief exploration of lying's potentially constructive uses borrowed from Judge Alex Kozinski's more detailed examination when *Alvarez* came before the Court of Appeals for the Ninth Circuit on its way to the

Supreme Court. Writing to explain why he voted to deny en banc review, Kozinski sang the praises of the everyday lies that could be criminalized if the government's theory that "'false statements of fact are always unprotected by the First Amendment'" prevailed.

An "ever-truthful utopia," Judge Kozinski insisted, would be "terrifying." The Stolen Valor Act would punish every misrepresentation about the coveted awards whether voiced in public or private, in a whisper or echoing through the mountains.

If lies were unprotected speech, Kozinski posited, a wide range of expression would be subject to criminal penalty: the "Jdater who falsely claims he's Jewish or the dentist who assures you it won't hurt a bit. Phrases such as 'I'm working late tonight, hunny [sic],' or ... 'I didn't inhale' could all be made into crimes. Without the robust protections of the First Amendment, the white lies, exaggerations and deceptions that are an integral part of human intercourse would become targets of censorship."

"For mortals," Kozinski asserted, "living means lying." Citing social science literature, Kozinski observed that Americans tell "somewhere between two and fifty lies each day." The Ninth Circuit dissenters, who would have granted a rehearing to the government and presumably then ruled to uphold the Stolen Valor Act, had argued that many untruths were not falsifiable and therefore could never be subject to criminal penalty. Not so, Kozinski responded: "If you tell a girl you love her in the evening and then tell your roommate she's a bimbo the next morning, and the two compare notes, someone's going to call you a liar" even though neither statement could be termed a "fact."[9]

Xavier Alvarez the Man

One may or may not agree with Judge Kozinski that living is lying, but for Xavier Alvarez it certainly was. Let's take a closer look at how and where he lied, and how he got caught.

The July 23, 2007, meeting of the Water Board was not the first time Alvarez had falsely asserted that he held the Medal of Honor. After his election, but before the Water Board met, Alvarez took a tour bus to visit a power plant. He asked Melissa Campbell—the power plant employee who was leading the tour—"Do you know who I am?" He quickly answered his own rhetorical question: "I am a Congressional Medal of Honor recipient."

Poor Alvarez, he chose the wrong audience. Melissa Campbell, a US Marine Corps veteran with ten years of service, doubted Alvarez's claim. As they boarded the tour bus, Alvarez had told Campbell they had a lot in common and that as a Marine he had spent twenty-five years in reconnaissance. Campbell found that strange, because she had never heard of anyone doing reconnaissance for so long. When he later told her about his medal, she recalled, "I about dropped the snacks all over the place. I'd rather meet a CMH winner than a rock star." She told Alvarez she was "in awe of him." She pulled up a list of the living Medal of Honor winners on her phone. His name was not on it. She immediately realized "this is a big deal. This is like against the law." At dinner that night, others on the tour praised Alvarez for his military service, which had ballooned to include the Silver Star, another honor covered by the Stolen Valor Act. Alvarez got the adulation he sought and a standing ovation.

Now Campbell's alarm bells were clanging. She thought the details Alvarez reported about the events leading to his awards resembled the plot of the Samuel Jackson film *Rules of Engagement*. When Alvarez started telling some of the guests about all the people he had killed, including children, that was too much. He was putting the Marine Corps in a bad light. So Campbell started asking him questions. Campbell reported Alvarez to the FBI because the details did not seem to add up.[10]

About one month later, Alvarez repeated the lie at his first Water Board meeting. The FBI, which had opened an investigation into Alvarez after Campbell complained, obtained a recording of the meeting. After Alvarez pleaded guilty in federal court to violating the Stolen Valor Act, the judge sentenced him to three years on probation and 416 hours of community service, and fined him $5,000 plus an additional $100 assessment.

The charges against Alvarez did not require the government to show what motivated his lies or even to speculate. But we might understand him and the meaning of his posing better from the perspective of the social utility of lies.

Personal autonomy, a First Amendment value, often leads people to lie to others or to themselves. "Speaking about oneself," Judge Kozinski observed, "is precisely when people are most likely to exaggerate, obfuscate, embellish, omit key facts or tell tall tales."[11] This is exactly what got Xavier Alvarez into trouble.

For example, people on dating sites often exaggerate or lie about their accomplishments, resumés, and physical attractiveness. If a man claims to be 6'1" tall but is only 5'7", is that a lie or an exaggeration? What if he is only 5'1" or if he is 6' even? What "truth police" would determine the difference between an exaggeration (protected by the Speech Clause) and a falsifiable statement of fact (unprotected under the government's theory about the Stolen Valor Act)?

Lies designed to put oneself in the best possible light, according to behavioral economist Daniel Ariely, enable the natural storytelling capacity of humans.[12] Sometimes lies allow us to experiment with different personae for public presentation, to reimagine ourselves in varied social contexts, or to explore what we want out of life. All of these conscious or unconscious motivations might apply to Xavier Alvarez.

Lies that facilitate a more satisfying self-presentation are not limited to words: Americans spend tens of billions of dollars each year to improve their appearance or, as some might put it, to deceive others about their height, age, financial status, and so forth. If these actions were understood to be expressive conduct, or what is known as symbolic speech (conduct intended to communicate a message that is likely to be understood), and the government established that lies are unprotected, then the mere wearing of a huge cubic zirconia ring might become a crime.

As with most things legal, treatment of the cubic zirconia ring would not be simple. Before we punished the ring-wearer, we would probably want to know whether she knew it was not a diamond, whether she owned an identical-looking diamond that she kept in a safe, or whether she wanted to communicate that she was wealthier than she really was. I would also like to know why she wore the diamond. Did she care how much money other people thought she had, and if so, why? Did she think the ring was a hoot, or did she hope the ring would help her marry a millionaire, or defraud one of a fortune?

Maybe Xavier Alvarez just craved a different life or a bit of respect, and regarded his lies as no more than puffery. We will never know because once he pleaded guilty in the trial court the facts were never developed in the courtroom. And even if the case had gone to trial, there would have been no need for the government to show what motivated Alvarez's deception. Under the Stolen Valor Act the plain fact of his false claim sufficed to establish his crime—which turned out to be an unsalvageable constitutional infirmity.

Why the Government Cared

Once it is established that a government regulation like the Stolen Valor Act inhibits protected speech based on its content, judicial inquiry turns to the government's interest in the subject matter of the infringement. Strict scrutiny analysis requires that the government establish a "compelling" or vital public interest in the problem the legislation has identified. No judge or justice doubted that preserving the sanctity of the highest military honors was such an interest.

The Congressional Medal of Honor, the nation's highest honor, was established in 1861. The Medal recognizes conspicuous bravery "at the risk of life and above and beyond the call of duty."[13] Only 3,476 military heroes received the Medal over the next century and a half. Since World War I, more than half of the honorees received the Medal posthumously. Many of them died trying to save others in their units on the battlefield.

By the turn of the twenty-first century an apparent groundswell of false claimants to the Medal had developed. In 2003 alone more than six hundred residents of Virginia falsely claimed to hold the Medal, likely inspired by the tax breaks the state offered to military heroes. The number was preposterous on its face. If six hundred Virginians actually held the Medal, they would have constituted 17 percent of all the individuals who had received it since 1861. What's more, a mere 132 Medal of Honor winners remained alive in 2003, only 4 of them in the state of Virginia. One-third of the people listed in *Who's Who* online who claimed they held the Medal of Honor were lying.

A spate of stories publicized false claimants to the Medal and similar though lesser-ranked honors including the Silver and Bronze Stars, the Purple Heart, and the Distinguished Service Cross. These included a judge who displayed two counterfeit Medals of Honor in his chambers, a Fox News military consultant, and a retired Marine Corps judge advocate. Congress passed the Stolen Valor Act in 2005 in an effort to stem the growing number, increasing brazenness, and harms of these false claims.

Congressional findings supporting the legislation pointed to tangible and intangible harms resulting from imposters' lies. Tangible harms included using the false claims to receive financial benefits such as consulting contracts, higher veterans' benefits and other perquisites, and income tax relief in some states, including Virginia. The intangible harms seemed equally serious. Bona fide Medal of Honor recipients protested that fraudulent claims debased their Medals. They felt as if the imposters had literally slapped them in the face.[14] All of these facts suggest that a compelling public interest led Congress to pass the Stolen Valor Act.

And so one may reasonably have read this far wondering why *Alvarez* was a paradigm-shifting case that deserves a full chapter in this book. As the legal community awaited the decision in *Alvarez*, many of us assumed that with such a heavy government interest, slight reason not to rein in false claimants, and so little social utility in the kind of lie Xavier Alvarez told, the government would win. If the government lost, we assumed the decision would be fairly clear-cut. I vividly recall my expectations, because I had been asked to conduct a law school faculty workshop on *Alvarez* when the decision came down. My expectations were wrong. That presentation led me to years of research on the relationship between lies and freedom of expression.

The Supreme Court Opinions in *United States* v. *Alvarez*

The Supreme Court issued its splintered decision in *Alvarez* on June 28, 2012, the end of the term, when the most highly anticipated opinions are generally released. Lawyers call a decision splintered when there are more than two opinions (normally a decision for the Court and a dissent) that together do not provide clear guidance about the Court's reasoning because no analysis has earned a majority of the justices' votes.

Three opinions issued in *Alvarez*, each using a different mode of analysis. In addition to Justice Kennedy's opinion for a three-person plurality, Justice Breyer (joined by Justice Elena Kagan) issued a concurrence. A concurrence is a separate opinion that agrees with the outcome that received the most votes in a case but applies different legal reasoning. Together, Kennedy's opinion and Breyer's concurrence provided a five-person majority on the central holding: the Stolen Valor Act was unconstitutional and was unconstitutionally applied to Xavier Alvarez. Justice Samuel Alito (joined by Justices Antonin Scalia and Clarence Thomas) dissented. Each opinion applied distinctive reasoning.

Justice Kennedy's opinion for the plurality forcefully repudiated the government's position that it had the power to control deception. The cases on which the government relied do not establish, Justice Kennedy declared, the "principle" the government urged the court to adopt, "that all proscriptions of false statements are exempt from exacting First Amendment scrutiny." Instead, the precedents, he showed, do not support the "broader proposition that false statements are unprotected when made to any person, at any time, in any context."

Most starkly, a law that "targets falsehood and nothing more," as the Stolen Valor Act did, violates the First Amendment. The court affirmed the

Ninth Circuit decision overturning the act and effectively overturning Alvarez's conviction under it.

In many ways the facts in *Alvarez* presented the best possible case for enforcing the statute because Alvarez had told, in Justice Kennedy's words, a "straight-out" intentional lie, with "no shades of meaning" that could support a different interpretation. He lied in a public meeting. However, he had neither benefited from his lie nor demonstrably harmed anyone.

The imposter who benefits from his lie came before the Tenth Circuit Court of Appeals in *United States* v. *Strandlof*, another Stolen Valor Act case decided about three weeks before the Supreme Court heard oral arguments in *Alvarez*. The Tenth Circuit upheld the Stolen Valor Act against a First Amendment challenge on very different facts. Rick Strandlof was a con man. Like Alvarez, he had never served in the armed forces. Posing as a decorated veteran and using an alias, Strandlof founded a veterans group that solicited donations. He raised money by promoting the false story that he had attended the United States Naval Academy, had been wounded in Iraq, and had been awarded both the Silver Star and a Purple Heart. Strandlof's case did not reach the Supreme Court, and the Supreme Court had no reason to consider the distinction between Rick Strandlof and Xavier Alvarez. *Strandlof* would have offered the "more" in addition to the bald-faced lie that was lacking in Alvarez's case, the absence of which troubled Justice Kennedy.

If mere falsehood, without more, of the sort Alvarez engaged in could be criminalized, there would be, Justice Kennedy wrote, "no limiting principle." The government would have "authority to compile a list of subjects" based on content "about which false statements are punishable." And the government would be able to punish lies "whether shouted from the rooftops or made in a barely audible whisper."

Many of Judge Kozinski's examples of lies in everyday life involved intimate relationships. Imagine if lies whispered in seduction or in sexual relations could result in arrest and prosecution. Well, many lies like that used to be punishable in criminal law (fornication and adultery laws) and civil law (alienation of affection or wrongful seduction). Modern constitutional understanding of privacy rights and individual liberty largely bars enforcement of such laws today.

Justice Breyer, concurring, conceded that the court had said or implied in the past that "false factual statements enjoy little First Amendment protection," but that did not mean "no protection at all." He suggested that the law should treat false statements about easily verifiable facts (like whether someone held the Medal of Honor) differently than it treats other kinds of false assertions, on which reasonable minds might differ. Still, he agreed with the plurality that the statute potentially implicated too much speech that should remain uncensored. And Justice Breyer warned that the act was susceptible to selective prosecution based on the imposter's political stance and how the imposter used the false claim. The dissenters, in contrast, could not imagine that the speaker's views would play any role in deciding whom to prosecute.

Justice Alito's dissent, joined by Justices Scalia and Thomas, would have upheld both the Stolen Valor Act and Alvarez's conviction under it because they read the precedents differently from Justices Kennedy and Breyer. Justice Alito agreed with the government that lies should be added to the categorical exclusions and removed from First Amendment protection. He opined that "as a general matter false factual statements possess no intrinsic First Amendment value," adding that "many kinds of false factual statements have long been proscribed without 'rais[ing] any Constitutional problem.'" Here, he pointed correctly to laws prohibiting fraud, perjury, and defamation, all of which were illegal before the American Revolution under British common law, and to more recent regulations including statutes making it a crime to deceive government officials or impersonate a government official, all of which survived the *Alvarez* decision. In support of his argument, Justice Alito quoted a string of nonbinding obiter dicta that dismissed the inherent value of falsehoods.

Justice Kennedy responded forcefully to the dissent's use of dicta about falsehoods. The exchange was in the tradition under which the justices circulate their opinions before they become public, and often use the published opinions for a dialogue among themselves.

Justice Kennedy cabined the court's earlier statements about deceptions the state could punish within several narrow categories. The comments on which the dissent relied, Justice Kennedy clarified, were all drawn from "cases about defamation, fraud, or some other legally cognizable harm associated with a false statement." Harmful falsehoods that could be regulated without offending the First Amendment include deception voiced "to effect a fraud or secure moneys or other valuable considerations," several types of material falsehoods made to government officials, and perjured testimony made under oath that undermines "the function . . . of the law," misleads policymakers, or "affect[s] the rights and liberties of others."

The court, Justice Kennedy wrote, had never endorsed the broad proposition that all falsehoods lack First Amendment protection and would not do so now. Indeed, its recent decisions repudiated as "startling and dangerous" invitations to expand the limited categories of unprotected speech. Recognizing a new category of unprotected speech based on its content would require "free-floating . . . ad hoc balancing of relative costs and benefits," an approach anathema to developing predictable legal doctrine.

Justice Kennedy emphasized the role of falsehoods in the freewheeling political debate at the heart of the Speech Clause. Rebuking the government and the dissenters for relying on obiter dicta, Justice Kennedy underscored that "some false statements are inevitable if there is to be an open and vigorous expression of views in public and private conversation, expression the First Amendment seeks to guarantee."

He reminded us that the classic "remedy for speech that is false is speech that is true. . . . The response . . . to the straight-out lie, the simple truth." And, Justice Kennedy said, as the law anticipates, the "ordinary course in a free society" of revealing deception had proven its effectiveness in the case before the court. When word of Alvarez's self-aggrandizing fabrication got out, the local press and people in the community pilloried him. Outraged community members posted online comments calling him "an idiot" and "a jerk." Local veterans protested. Fellow board members demanded Alvarez resign. He did not.

No Road Map

All of the justices agreed that the First Amendment prohibits the government from becoming the arbiter of truth.

That is about all they agreed on. The splintered grounds for the opinions meant that *Alvarez* failed to fulfill one of the Supreme Court's traditional functions: to guide lower courts and legislatures.

The justices did not even clarify what class of constitutional right a right to lie belongs in. Those who held for Xavier Alvarez did not address whether the right he claimed was "fundamental," which would have put it on the same plane as the specified individual rights spelled out in various amendments. If the court had labeled a right to lie (or even a right to lie in some circumstances) as fundamental, the required standard of review would have been clear—strict scrutiny applies to all unadulterated speech rights. (A lesser standard applies when speech is merged with non-expressive conduct.) Strict scrutiny would have made it nigh on impossible to regulate lies in the public square.

Having sidestepped labeling the right to lie as fundamental (like speech generally) or "quasi-suspect" (like gender bias under the Fourteenth Amendment), the justices whose votes comprised a majority remained unable to agree on a standard of review for lower courts to apply in disputes involving restrictions on verifiably false statements of fact. We need to briefly venture into what may seem like a highly technical discussion of legal maneuvers because the standard of review applied to a First Amendment controversy usually determines the outcome of a case. The nuances will prove significant as we look at lies from different angles in subsequent chapters.

The distinctions in *Alvarez* largely centered on how strong an interest the government had to show to justify infringing on false speech. Each of the three opinions applied a different standard. Adding to the complexity of what follows, none of the opinions used the classical formulation of the standard to which the author referred.

Justice Alito's dissent rejected the notion that the First Amendment protected Alvarez's lies, which left the dissent free to use the most deferential form of review, rational basis. Rational basis review requires only that the state act within a "legitimate" area of interest and have a rationale for its actions. While Alito did not identify the standard he applied, he stated that "Congress reasonably concluded" that lies about Medals of Honor inflicted "real harm" on the actual recipients.

Implicitly, the dissenters accepted the proposition that a different sort of lie, one that did not inflict harm, might have First Amendment protection. And if ascertaining the truth were less straightforward than establishing who won a military award, as with statements about "history, science, and similar matters," Alito asked: "How certain must it be that a statement is false before the ban may be upheld? And who should make that calculation?" In that case, a higher standard than rationality would surely be required.

Courts applying rational basis uphold legislative choices even if reasonable minds could differ, making the test extremely easy for the government to satisfy. That should have been enough to end Justice Alito's inquiry.

But Alito continued, creating a puzzle. The act, he said, needed some additional conditions to protect speech—such as an intent requirement and an exception for "dramatic performances, satire, parody, hyperbole, or the like"—and Alito proceeded to read those limitations into the statute's silence. Doing so violated the rule that courts do not legislate. After imputing those limitations to the Stolen Valor Act, Alito declared the act "narrow," meaning that it would not affect too much protected speech.

Alito's inquiry into narrowness muddled the standard of review. Rational basis review would not normally ask whether the regulation is "narrowly crafted" to avoid limiting more speech than is necessary to achieve the governmental goal. Narrowness is a prong of strict scrutiny analysis.

In contrast, Justice Breyer's concurrence applied his preferred alternative to strict scrutiny, a form of balancing that he calls "proportionality." Proportionality is essentially intermediate scrutiny, which as the name suggests is easier for the government to satisfy than strict scrutiny. The state must establish that it has a "substantial" interest in regulating speech, an undefined zone between "compelling" and "legitimate."

Justice Kennedy's plurality opinion used a more stringent test than Alito or Breyer, but stopped short of announcing that strict scrutiny was necessary. Strict scrutiny requires the government to establish a compelling interest in solving a real problem. Justice Kennedy referred to "compelling interests" in close proximity to terms like "exacting" and "most exacting" scrutiny. The hodgepodge of words drawn from different constitutional standards created confusion over what test Justice Kennedy was using. If the standard of review for deceptive speech is more forgiving than strict scrutiny (that is, not "strictly" strict scrutiny), then the plurality is signaling that falsehood is not on the same constitutional plane as other protected speech.

Ultimately, all of the justices agreed that Congress had sound enough reasons under the standard each applied to address the stolen valor problem. That is hardly surprising in light of Kennedy's position. A government interest that satisfies the most demanding requirement applied—whether it proves "compelling" or merely "substantial"—will obviously also prove legitimate.

However, the justices disagreed about whether the act survived the other elements of any standards more demanding than rational basis.

Justices Kennedy and Breyer found the statute unconstitutional for several reasons. Among other things, less restrictive alternatives to criminal penalty existed. Truthful counter-speech would effectively correct prevaricators.

In addition, Justices Kennedy and Breyer both concluded that the act lacked a limiting principle: it reached too much protected speech unrelated to the statute's goals. For instance, the act did not require that the false claim be a serious one; it might reach theatrical performances or humor—exactly the issue Alito cured by fiat. It might also reach the sort of private braggadocio that concerned Kozinski and Breyer. The act was overbroad, a finding that rendered it unconstitutional. Overbreadth is the opposite of narrowness.

Most critically, the statute did not require proof of harm or benefit. A "more finely tailored statute" might be limited, Justice Breyer suggested, by requiring the government show specific harm or be limited to "contexts where such lies are most likely to cause harm." "Harm" means an injury of a type the law can measure and compensate, not the heartache or regret that may follow a personal relationship that later turns out to have been premised on deceit.

Justice Kennedy agreed. The plurality opinion intimated that the government might be able to constitutionally regulate falsehoods if it could show what I will refer to as "something more" (the converse of the "nothing more" and "without more" than falsity held inadequate in *Alvarez*). However, as with the level of scrutiny, the court failed to provide directions about what kind of harm and what level of harm the government must show to sustain a law that criminalizes verifiable factual falsehoods.

The court left legislators, judges, and lawyers asking questions that run though this book: What kind of harms or ill-gotten benefits might suffice to justify government regulation of lies? And, if falsehoods are less bald-faced than Xavier Alvarez's lie, what arbiter of truth might interpret the words and enforce restrictions on falsehoods without offending the First Amendment?

Epilogue

Xavier Alvarez won his case, but that vindication did not end his legal woes. He achieved notoriety, just not of the kind he envisioned. Shortly after Alvarez was arrested on federal charges of violating the Stolen Valor Act, he was charged with insurance fraud, misappropriation of public funds, and grand theft in Pomona Superior Court. He had fraudulently filed for health insurance benefits from the Water Board for his ex-wife, who was not a qualified dependent. The crimes might never have come to light if Alvarez had not already been under the spotlight for fabricating a distinguished military career. In 2009 Alvarez was convicted, sentenced to five years in prison, and barred from holding public office in the future. Alvarez was released from Calipatria State Prison in 2012 after the Supreme Court heard oral argument in his stolen valor case.

In 2013 Congress passed a revised Stolen Valor Act, signed into law by President Barack Obama. It remedied the constitutional infirmities of the 2005 act overturned in *Alvarez*. The 2013 statute criminalizes only "fraudulent" false claims to have received enumerated high military decorations. Fraud requires knowledge of falsehood and intent to deceive, two areas on which the earlier act was silent. The 2013 act also responded to Justice Kennedy's instruction that to survive a First Amendment challenge, a regulation on false speech must target something "more" than falsehood alone. It should identify the harm the falsehood caused others, or the benefit that redounded to the liar. The 2013 act targets the imposter who lies about a military decoration "in order to obtain money, property, or other tangible benefit."[15] If it had been in effect a few years earlier, it would have reached the con man Rick Strandlof, but not Xavier Alvarez.

Justice Kennedy reminded us that while few would find any saving grace in Xavier Alvarez's false claims, lies Kennedy called "contemptible," the First Amendment "protects the speech we detest as well as the speech we embrace." With remarkable self-constraint, he explained that statutes restricting speech "must be judged by the sometimes inconvenient principles of the First Amendment." Yes, it can be "inconvenient," even frustrating, or enraging that our society is unable to silence speech virtually no one wants to hear. That is one cost of freedom.

CHAPTER 3

Incredible Lies: Defamation and Birtherism

I n 2011, Jerome Corsi, a supporter of Donald Trump's, published a book he claimed provided definitive evidence that Barack Obama did not have a Hawaii birth certificate, could not prove he was born in the United States, and therefore was not eligible to serve as president. Despite abundant citations, the book was bereft of any factual foundation. A defamation case followed, but it was not the one you might expect. Instead of President Obama suing Corsi, Corsi and his publisher sued *Esquire Magazine* over an online column that parodied Corsi's remote relationship with the truth. They sought more than $120 million in damages.

In plain English, defamation is a nasty lie that damages someone's reputation because it may be impossible to counter with the traditional more and better speech. Defamation law allows individuals whose reputations have been harmed by factual falsehoods to sue the defamer for written ("libel") or verbal ("slander") statements. The doctrine offers the hope of constraining a class of harmful public lies.

The law provides this civil remedy because it recognizes that the speaker, whether the classic newspaper or the contemporary social media star, may reach a broader audience with untruths than the victims of defamation may ever hope to attract for their rebuttal. The speaker is also advantaged by a head start. The Supreme Court summed up the practical dilemma: "The truth rarely catches up with a lie."[1]

Wait a minute, you might say, this seems to be exactly the opposite of what the plurality in *United States* v. *Alvarez* assured us: that more and better speech is the preferred constitutional remedy to lies, and that counterspeech works. You'd be right.

But defamation raises distinct legal questions that were not at issue in *Alvarez*. Xavier Alvarez lied about himself and did not damage anyone directly. The defamer lies about others and damages their standing in the community. In both settings, however, the Supreme Court has stressed that the law will not provide recompense for speech that does not actually harm someone. To date, the court has not articulated a general principle governing what kind of harm or how severe it must be before the government or a private person can prevail against a liar.

Although a defamation lawsuit arises between two private parties, reliance on courts to settle the dispute involves government action, rendering the First Amendment applicable. Victims who bring defamation claims rely on state laws and courts to restore their good names and to force the dishonest speaker to pay them damages. Defamation is among the limited types of expression that are said to be categorically excluded from the protections the Speech Clause offers. Removing defamation from the definition of constitutionally protected expression transforms the legal posture of the speech. If the Speech Clause applied, it would be unconstitutional to regulate an untrue statement based on its content alone.

When the law considers defamation, it exercises a sleight of hand: the state initially uses content to determine whether the First Amendment applies. Through the courts, the state assesses whether the statement contains a verifiably false fact and plausibly meets the definition of libel or slander. If the statement is factually false, standard First Amendment protections no longer apply. Instead, the court uses special legal rules designed for defamation cases that strive to balance the First Amendment's commitment to robust expression with private reputational interests that depend on constraining falsehoods.

An inevitable tension exists in the United States between state laws that penalize defamation and constitutional protections for free speech. As we have seen, the Speech Clause protects the free flow of ideas and opinions. In stark contrast, defamation law discourages a particular kind of speech based on its content—speech that harms others by spreading false statements of fact about them. The promise of defamation law as a permissible defensive weapon against public lies that harm others regularly runs head-on into constitutional principles.

After setting out the unique fundamentals of US defamation doctrine, this chapter explores its complexities through four powerful episodes: the libel case Corsi and his publisher brought against another author and publisher arising out of the birtherism controversy; an imaginary scenario in which President Obama might have sued the proponents of birtherism (he did not); the legal implications of President Trump's baseless charges that Joe Scarborough murdered one of his congressional aides; and a group of pending cases that involve both the misuse and intended use of defamation suits.

Legal Building Blocks: *New York Times* v. *Sullivan*

The New York Times Company v. *Sullivan*, which the Supreme Court decided in 1964, remains the seminal case about the relationship between the First Amendment and defamation claims. In it, the court reversed a large jury award to L. B. Sullivan, an elected official in Montgomery, Alabama, who supervised the city's police force during a period rife with racial tension and civil rights demonstrations. Sullivan asserted that prominent civil rights leaders had libeled him by implication (he was recognizable, though not named) in an advertisement they had purchased in the *Times*.

The court posited that Sullivan was no ordinary citizen. He had to meet a higher standard of proof to prevail: "Public men, are, as it were, public property" who subject themselves to public criticism by virtue of their status.[2]

Sullivan held that the First Amendment limits the state's power to impose liability for defamation of a public official. Among other things, the court reasoned, the Constitution protects the right of the governed to criticize those who govern them. *Sullivan* imposed a new standard for cases involving defamation of public officials (proof of "actual malice") that would be much harder to satisfy than the common law rules governing defamation cases, as I will explain in more detail below.

The court reasoned that a legal regime that made it too easy for the powerful to prevail when they sue for defamation violates free speech by exposing speakers to too much risk. Damages awarded to victims of defamation in a civil lawsuit burden speech just as much as a fine levied by the government. Both "chill" speech, meaning they discourage expression. The mere threat of a lawsuit hovering in the background when facts are unclear could easily dissuade writers, publishers, and other speakers from sharing information of public concern about government officials. Just like criminal fines and sentences, civil damages threaten to make those who speak about public figures or matters of public concern think twice before articulating their views. Fear of damages may dissuade citizens from expressing their views at all.

The balance comes out differently when factual falsehoods defame people who are not public figures. In those cases, judicial remedies for defamation are justified by the argument that falsehoods adversely affecting individual reputations cause so much social damage that the harm outweighs the constitutional commitment to unbridled expression. Thus the legal test, described below, is much easier for the average person who has been defamed to satisfy: merely careless or negligent statements could be sufficient to impose liability.

Balancing protection of public figures against free speech, *Sullivan* held that safeguarding vigorous debate outweighs other concerns. In the court's view, the "breathing space" essential to vigorous discussion makes "the erroneous statement . . . inevitable in free debate." Our democracy, the court explained, is premised on the idea that energetic debate on public issues will lead to optimal conclusions. While some may believe this confidence is "folly," as Judge Learned Hand famously stated, "we have staked upon it our all." *Sullivan* underscored that it is fundamental to democracy that public debate be "uninhibited, robust, and wide-open."[3]

Writing for the court in *Sullivan*, Justice William Brennan explained the theory behind constitutional protection for falsehoods in public debate. He relied in part on John Stuart Mill's argument in *On Liberty* that truth is illuminated when forced to collide with falsehood. Moreover, a few factual errors, like some details in the civil rights ad in the *Times* (for example, how many times Dr. Martin Luther King Jr. had been arrested in Alabama, what song the protesters were singing), do not render an entire statement false and therefore defamatory.

The court expressly held that speech containing some "factual error," "half-truths," or "misinformation" does not "forfeit" constitutional protections. It could not be otherwise because, the court reminded us, the First Amendment does not contemplate "any test of truth . . . especially one that puts the burden of proving truth on the speaker."[4]

What Falsehoods Defame?

What kinds of falsehoods are so outrageously harmful that the state should inhibit them? In the old days, a false assertion that a woman was unchaste, that a man had contracted venereal disease, or that either was insane almost always amounted to defamation. Other examples include falsely accusing someone of beating a spouse, being a rapist, or being involved with organized crime.

False statements of fact may be direct or indirect and may be aimed at professional reputation as well as personal attributes. For instance, accusing a halal or kosher butcher of selling pork predictably harms the butcher's reputation and causes customers to flee. Like a direct accusation, an indirect slur can have a powerful impact. Implying that the butcher sells pork by saying "I saw the pig farmer's van unloading in back of the butcher shop" is likely to decimate the butcher's reputation in the community he serves as much as saying "He foists pork on unsuspecting customers." Today, the loose hyperbole rampant on social media provides fodder for defamation actions, at least if the speaker can be identified.

Birtherism I: *Farah* v. *Esquire Magazine*

The multilayered defamation case brought by Jerome Corsi and his publisher in 2011 responded to an online *Esquire* article about Corsi's book on birtherism. The conspiratorial theory known as birtherism took root in 2008 when Barack Obama was running for, and then elected, president. It is the unfounded assertion that Obama was born in Kenya, and therefore was not qualified for his office because the Constitution requires that the president be "a natural Born citizen." In fact, two different forms of Obama's birth certificate, confirmation by Hawaiian officials, and two birth announcements in local newspapers on August 13, 1961, established that he had been born in Honolulu. Yet birtherism continued throughout the Obama presidency, providing a vehicle for right-wingers who mourned the fading dominance of White America. It retains vitality in some circles today.

The Main Players

No one ran with birtherism more than Donald J. Trump, beginning well before he became a candidate for public office. After Obama assumed office in 2009, Trump sought every opportunity to expound upon the birther lie, in the words of one journalist, "wielding his trademark innuendos and falsehoods." Fox News jumped on board, featuring Trump and his slippery statements intended to evade responsibility for his charges: "He doesn't have a birth certificate . . . maybe religion, maybe it says he's a Muslim; I don't know."

Trump announced on a Fox News show in March 2011, "I have people that have been studying it and they cannot believe what they are finding" in classic Trump deniable prose. This posturing suggests knowledge of facts others do not have access to, while allowing the speaker to duck if the allegations prove unfounded: "It's not me, I'm relying on what someone else said." Such maneuvering transformed Trump from a multiple-bankrupt real estate developer / casino operator and reality TV personality into a pseudo-respectable political commentator. Political strategist Dick Morris asserted, it "legitimizes his candidacy."[5]

Finally, on April 27, 2011, in the face of repeated birther attacks, President Obama released a copy of his Hawaiian "long-form" birth certificate, which stated he was born in Honolulu. The long-form birth certificate, unique to Hawaii, requires information about every newborn that enables the state to determine whether a person is at least 50 percent native Hawaiian and qualifies for programs benefiting indigenous people. Its release should have put the entire matter to rest.

But it did not. Instead, Trump, echoed and promoted by Fox News, went all in on birtherism during the 2012 Republican primary season, in which Trump tested the waters but never became a candidate. By 2016, when Trump sought and won the Republican nomination and then the presidency, he had perfected the strategy for espousing birtherism that he would resort to in many contexts: tell a big, bold, shameless lie and count on conservatives to repeat it until people take it as truth.

Three weeks after Obama released his long-form birth certificate, WND Books published Jerome Corsi's *Where's the Birth Certificate? The Case That Barack Obama Is Not Eligible to Be President*. WND Books, a wholly owned subsidiary of WorldNetDaily (WND), belongs to Joseph Farah, who founded WND as a for-profit entity in 1999. Farah is a former mainstream journalist who had tried and failed to turn a Sacramento newspaper into a fundamentalist Christian organ. The Southern Poverty Law Center has labeled WND an "extremist group" dedicated to "paranoid, gay-hating, conspiratorial and apocalyptic visions . . . from the fringes of the far-right and fundamentalist worlds."[6]

Jerome Corsi found a natural home writing for WND. Corsi, who holds a PhD in political science from Harvard, worked in 2016 with now-convicted and pardoned felon Roger Stone to help elect Donald Trump as president. Stone had gained the national spotlight when he was widely credited with organizing the pro-Bush "Brooks Brothers riot" that disrupted ballot counting in Miami-Dade County, Florida, during the contested 2000 presidential election. Later, the right-wing Regnery Publishing released Corsi's *Unfit for Command*, the basis for the so-called swiftboater attacks on Senator John Kerry's military service when he headed the Democratic ticket in 2004. The swiftboaters falsely claimed that instead of being a war hero, Kerry was a coward and a fraud. Although *Unfit for Command* made it to the *New York Times*'s best seller list, neutral reviewers excoriated Corsi's work as riddled with inaccuracies that his numerous citations failed to substantiate.

Together, Corsi and Farah made birtherism a cornerstone of the WND site, continuing their attacks even after the release of Obama's long-form birth certificate. The WND site trumpeted Corsi's book on Obama's birth certificate as "**The book that proves Obama's ineligible**" (emphasis in original).[7]

The Facts

The day after *Where's the Birth Certificate?* appeared, *Esquire Magazine*'s online *Politics Blog* published journalist Mark Warren's article entitled "BREAKING: Jerome Corsi's Birther Book Pulled from Shelves!" Warren revealed what he called a "stunning development." Just one day after publication, the story said, publisher Farah announced that all two hundred thousand copies of the book (which was already for sale in bookstores and online) would be pulled from the shelves and pulped. Warren also announced that Farah would refund the purchase price to customers who had already obtained the book.

In case anyone would believe that a publisher would shred a book that had just been released, Warren peppered the story with clues to his humorous intent. He quoted Farah as having said the book "contains what I now believe to be factual inaccuracies . . . I cannot in good conscience publish it and expect anyone to believe it." The language used in reporting Farah's reaction to recent developments offered further clues that the article was not meant to be credited as factual. An anonymous source, Warren wrote, "said that Farah was 'rip-shit'" when Obama released his long-form birth certificate, "thus resolving the matter of Obama's legitimacy 'for anybody with a brain.'" And Farah reportedly "tore [Corsi] a new one," lambasting him: "We don't want to look like fucking idiots, you know? Look, at the end of the day, bullshit is bullshit." Conventional journalism usually avoids such language.

Warren embedded numerous additional clues in his column. The top of the post showed the Drudge Siren, a symbol of the right-wing scandal-mongering *Drudge Report*, with the tag "Drudge Without Context." The column also referenced a nonexistent book attributed to Corsi titled *Capricorn One* that charged that the entire 1969 moon landing had been faked; *Capricorn One* was the title of a 1978 film starring O. J. Simpson about a fake landing on Mars.

About ninety minutes after Warren's piece appeared on *Politics Blog*, *Esquire* updated the site to clear up any misunderstandings: "*For those who didn't figure it out yet and the many on Twitter for whom it took a while*: We committed satire this morning." It declared that the Warren article was not true and referred readers to "serious" articles in *Esquire* about birtherism. The satire, *Esquire* explained, responded to the lack of remorse by an author and publisher who accused the president of fraud, even though the book's "core premise and reason to exist [had been] gutted by the news cycle several weeks" earlier after Obama's long-form birth certificate was released. The "despicable" claim about President Obama, the update stated, is not premised on "reality," but is designed "to hold their terribly gullible audience captive to their lies."

The Legal Dispute

Despite *Esquire*'s disclaimer that it never intended Warren's article to be taken seriously, Farah and Corsi sued Warren and the magazine for defamation and more in the District of Columbia. They sought over $100 million in actual damages and over $20 million in punitive damages.

The federal courts made short work of the lawsuit, known as *Farah* v. *Esquire Magazine*. The trial court dismissed the complaint, meaning there was no need to even conduct a trial. The judge found that the blog was fully protected satire—immune to a defamation suit. The Court of Appeals for the District of Columbia, often called the most important court in the country next to the Supreme Court, affirmed the dismissal. Its opinion provides guidance about how to assess defamation claims.

A person suing for defamation must establish four elements of the offense. The first element has always been a verifiably false statement of fact concerning the subject of the communication. If speakers can show that what they said is true, by definition no defamation occurred. The remaining required elements of a defamation claim are: second, the speaker "published" the falsehood by sharing it with at least one other person; third, the speaker either intended to mislead or was sufficiently careless to be held accountable; and fourth, the alleged victim of defamation has suffered harm that cannot be assuaged by trying to convince people of the truth.

Truth offers a complete defense in almost every jurisdiction, regardless of whether the case is heard in federal or state court. The defense does not require the "whole truth and nothing but the truth" that witnesses swear to provide when they testify. The truth defense in defamation cases only requires that the "gist" of the statement must be true, even if some immaterial details were incorrect.

Defamation should not be measured by a "gotcha" aimed at one part of a statement, as Justice Scalia once explained. Suppose a newspaper reports that a person has committed thirty-five burglaries, while he has actually committed only thirty-four. If false, the statement would be defamatory. However, it is not false under defamation law, because it is "substantially true," marred only by a minor factual falsehood. The statement is substantially true because it truthfully indicates that the person is a habitual burglar. The precise number of burglaries he committed does not materially change the truthfulness of the allegation. The average reader will not care whether the burglar committed thirty-four or thirty-five burglaries.[8]

The gist approach supports finding truthfulness, but not falsehood. For example, an edited series of statements by a political candidate taken out of context may be materially misleading even though the candidate made each of the statements. If the resulting false impression is defamatory, the gist should be found false despite verifiable facts embedded within it.

However, verifiable falsehood by itself will not necessarily lead to legal accountability. The Supreme Court indicated as much in *United States* v. *Alvarez*, where it warned, "Falsity alone may not suffice to bring the speech outside the First Amendment."[9] What else is needed?

It seems defamation's categorical removal from First Amendment requirements is not comprehensive. Since *Sullivan*, the Supreme Court has layered some additional constitutionally mandated safeguards for speakers on top of the common law. To be defamatory a statement must be reasonably

understood as stating false facts, and those facts must be reasonably expected to harm the subject's good standing. Before a court can find a speaker
liable for defamation, the speaker's words must "reasonably impl[y] false
and defamatory facts." The falsehood must be "reasonably capable of defamatory meaning" that would harm the subject's personal or professional
reputation.[10]

The defendant's mental state is also at issue. In a traditional defamation
action, courts ask if the speaker was careless regarding the inaccuracy. If a
public figure was defamed, courts using the higher *Sullivan* standard ask
whether the speaker intentionally misstated or acted recklessly enough to
find actual malice.

In *Alvarez*, Justice Kennedy expanded on why US courts had modified
traditional defamation law to make it compatible with the First Amendment's guarantees. The rule that a defamatory statement must be knowing
or reckless "exists to allow more speech, not less."[11]

In *Farah* the appeals court focused on defamation's constitutional requirements, under which "reasonably" is the critical word. A factual falsehood cannot "reasonably" disgrace the target unless it is believable. If the
falsehood is transparent, clearly offered in jest, or literally incredible, then
no one would believe it. If no one believes the false fact, the statement cannot cause harm.

The more over the line the false fact, the more the speaker is protected
against a claim that the lie harmed its target. The highest court in Wyoming
has lamented, "We now say that the more outrageous, vile, vulgar, humiliat-
ing and ridiculous the publication, the more it is protected. . . . If it is outrageous enough, it is 'all right.'"[12] Practicing attorneys who advise media
clients have told me that they increasingly help clients find the precise point
at which their comedic intent becomes clear enough to protect against a
defamation lawsuit. The legal doctrine seems to encourage purveyors of factual falsehoods to make their statements appear more removed from any
factual basis and ever more fantastical in order to find shelter in the First
Amendment.

In one famous example, no one would believe that a drunk Jerry Falwell Sr., the evangelical preacher and founder of Liberty University, committed incest with his mother in an outhouse. Yet that was the claim that led
Falwell to sue *Hustler* for libel and emotional distress based on a parody of a
long-running Campari ad campaign in which sexual innuendo comprised

the key element. The ads all featured celebrities sharing the "first time" they "tasted Campari." In the fake ad, *Hustler* quoted Falwell reminiscing about his "first time" with his mother: "My first time was in an outhouse . . . I never really expected to make it with Mom, but then after she showed all the other guys in town such a good time, I figured 'What the hell?' . . . we were drunk off our God-fearing asses on Campari."

When the Supreme Court decided the case in 1988, it held that no matter how much the parody distressed Falwell, no matter how "gross and repugnant" it seemed to most observers, the First Amendment protected the satirical ad because "it could not have reasonably been interpreted as stating actual facts" about Falwell. No reasonable person would believe that teetotaling Falwell got drunk, much less that he had sex with his mother and, to top it off, in an outhouse.[13]

A court must examine the precise statement, the context surrounding the statement, and the statement's reasonable meaning given the context. A claim made outside the context of defamation helps put different kinds of untruths into perspective. President Kennedy did not expect anyone to take him literally when he proudly proclaimed at the Berlin Wall, "Ich bin ein Berliner." Of course, everyone knew that Kennedy was not actually a Berliner. He used rhetorical hyperbole effectively to show his fellowship with the East Germans trapped behind the Berlin Wall and longing for freedom in 1963. As far as I know, no one accused Kennedy of lying.

In contrast, pernicious hyperbole may shelter the most noxious statements from legal consequences, as happened in a defamation case arising from online slut-shaming of a high school student. A Facebook post concocted a tale in which the teenage girl had contracted AIDS in Africa while "fucking a horse" and "screw[ing] a baboon." Devastating as this failed adolescent humor was to its victim, a court ruled that no libel occurred because no one would be so foolish as to think these events really happened.[14]

Daily life requires us to use common sense. Every day we distinguish the vigorous epithet or hyperbolic claim from the truth. No one purchasing a commodity whose price is based on weight should believe that "this bag" literally "weighs a ton." Even "the most careless reader," the Supreme Court observed, must have understood that an extremely unreasonable real estate developer described as a "blackmailer" due to his uncompromising stance in negotiations was not being accused of committing the crime of blackmail. The term "blackmailer" was metaphorical—rhetorical hyperbole, not defamation.[15]

Common rhetorical methods signal "I don't expect you to believe this." Beyond express disclaimers or flags indicating that "this is not to be taken as a factual statement," such signals can include placement, outlandish details, and elements of style, such as the crude ("rip him a new one") or very informal language (he was "rip-shit") featured in Warren's article about Corsi's book.

Satire shares with defamation law the goal of providing the weak a weapon against the powerful. Since ancient times, writers have used satire to critique governments and oligarchs. In ancient Greece, Aristophanes's biting plays reportedly led to his prosecution for slander. Even then, the court held that satire was protected: no law prohibited slander in a performance. Similarly, humor gave punch to Honoré Daumier's caricatures of wealth and high society in nineteenth-century France. Protecting satirical critiques of this sort lies at the heart of First Amendment concerns.

Social commentary grounded in truth is a mainstay of parody and satire, which often start with verifiable facts and then take off into parts unknown. Readers of the satirical news outlet *The Onion* routinely got confused about whether stories were real. Many observers have noted that as government officials have exploded (my own hyperbole) expectations about how world leaders behave, it has become much more challenging than it used to be for comedians like Stephen Colbert or the *Daily Show*'s Trevor Noah, who focus on current events, to distinguish their jokes from reality. Comedian John Oliver has given up joking. His current show, *Last Week Tonight*, resembles a weekly news magazine, only it's humorous and often goes into greater depth.

If readers were not completely up to date, they might not be able to easily discern whether the following lead was truth or satire: the day after President Trump tweeted that he might postpone the 2020 elections, his press secretary condemned China's imposition of a yearlong delay in Hong Kong's voting. It's true, but it could easily have come from *The Onion*.

If the news is at least as bizarre as any story a comedian can imagine, how can one signal "This story is a joke"? The risk that readers will think a joke is a truthful account of breaking developments explains why the *New Yorker* clearly labels columnist Andy Borowitz's satirical takes on the news as "Not the News," followed by another disclaimer, "Satire from the Borowitz Report."

The preposterous quotes that proliferated in a newspaper article pillorying a judge and a prosecutor clearly indicated a parody was afoot. The piece, titled "Stop the Madness," landed in my inbox, sent by a children's rights advocate who framed it as an alarming story about an out of control Texas juvenile justice system. The article attributed the following comment to a Texas judge who was sentencing a six-year-old: "It's time for us to stop treating [children] like children." Continuing, it quoted the prosecutor explaining why the state had not pursued the case in adult court: "Even in Texas there are some limits." When the officials sued the alternative newspaper in which the article appeared for libel, the state's highest court found the story too incredible to be believed. It explained that a "superficial degree of plausibility" is the very "hallmark of satire." No harm done, it concluded, and thus no defamation case.

Who are the hypothetical reasonable readers the courts assume can sort out hyperbole, satire, opinion, and more from statements offered as facts? Reasonable people may be defined differently in different legal contexts. The reasonable reader in a defamation case processes information with "care and prudence." That reader is "a person of ordinary intelligence" who is presumed to know the context of the speaker's comments, to be able to grasp the speaker's signals about whether the comments should be taken literally, and to have "some feel for the nuances of law and language."[16]

A legal construct dominant in first-year law school classes for many years posited a reasonable person who rode the Clapham bus to and from central London. That fictional citizen presumably had a basic education and recognizable middle-of-the road views. It is far more difficult to imagine that reasonable person in the contemporary United States. Who are reasonable people in a nation divided over what is true based in large part on where they get their information? Do they get news from the *Washington Post* and NPR? From Fox and Newsmax? Only from Facebook? Or not at all?

In addition to assuming that the recipient of the speech is reasonably competent and informed, the law safeguards speakers by giving the reasonable reader time for "careful reflection." Observers don't always immediately grasp hyperbolic or satirical intent when exposed to material intended to sting like bees. That has been a risk since at least 1729 when Jonathan Swift's *A Modest Proposal*—now taught as a model of satire—was initially condemned. Readers thought Swift was seriously recommending that Irish children be sold as meat to alleviate poverty and starvation. Today, all of the Supreme Court justices agree that the risk of audience confusion does not deprive the satirist of his defense.

Subsequent clarifications like the one *Esquire* offered about Corsi's book are common—one was issued about "Stop the Madness," the article about the sentencing of the six-year-old girl discussed above. The newspaper had responded to the initial complaint from the judge and prosecutor with a second article. The paper offered: "A clue for our cerebrally challenged readers who thought the story was real: It wasn't. It was a joke. We made it up. Not even Judge Whitten, we hope, would throw a 6-year-old girl in the slammer for writing a book report." To underscore the point, they added: "Unfortunately, some people—commonly known as 'clueless' or 'Judge Darlene Whitten'—did not get . . . the joke."[17] Such postscripts presumably fall within the window for reasonable reflection defamation law grants readers.

In *Farah* v. *Esquire*, the court concluded that Warren's satirical article could not reasonably be construed as offering verifiable truths. "Despite its literal falsity," the court reiterated, "satirical speech enjoys First Amendment protection." If satire cannot be reasonably interpreted as stating actual facts, it cannot constitute defamation. Stinging humor receives constitutional protection so that speakers are free to use the manner of expression they think will make their point most powerfully.

Although Joseph Farah conceded that when he initially saw the *Esquire* post he thought it was "poorly executed parody," responses to Warren's piece indicated that many people took it at face value. People contacted bookstores, bookstores and journalists contacted Farah, and stores started removing the book from shelves. The commotion immediately following Warren's post led *Esquire* to issue its follow-up disclaimer. Farah and Corsi claimed their reputations had been sullied. The outpouring of responses that appeared to take the *Esquire* piece seriously provided more proof of damage than is usual in defamation litigation where the harm is often reasonably likely rather than proven.

Still, the court found that neither Farah nor Corsi had been harmed. It assumed that the reasonable reader of *Esquire*'s blog knew the political context and was familiar with the blog, its style, and its earlier parodies. *Esquire*'s audience knew who Corsi was; readers recognized that he and WND were leading provocateurs in the birtherism movement. No one who possessed that information would believe that Farah voluntarily pulled the book on the very same day he had so triumphantly announced that its appearance would resolve President Obama's status once and for all. If some people had initially taken Warren's article on the *Esquire* blog as factual, that was not an insurmountable legal problem, because people are often initially taken in by satire before they have time to reflect.

The court was unimpressed that some readers apparently took Warren's article at face value: the contents "defie[d] common sense." The contrafactual and entirely fictitious developments in the blog were, the court concluded, simply "incredible." To the extent that some readers believed Warren presented verifiable facts rather than hyperbolic humor, they revealed themselves as especially vulnerable and even clueless. Those readers did not live up to their responsibility to code all the signals that Warren was joking.

Does this mean that readers who were taken in were less than "reasonable"? Perhaps. But the standard is not the most careless, or vulnerable, reader. It is the well-informed person.

Information siloes make the well-informed reader standard particularly intriguing in a case like *Farah*. Farah's complaint alleged that some 25 percent of Americans believed that the birth certificates President Obama shared were fraudulent. That quarter of the population—a significant minority—was presumably susceptible to Corsi's unsubstantiated arguments. If they followed the WND blog, those readers were unlikely to immediately perceive that Warren was making fun of them as well as of Corsi and Farah.

The parties also disputed whether *Esquire*'s subsequent disclaimer expressed opinions or constituted a second libelous attack, a distinction that can be difficult to draw. If opinion, it should not be construed as stating a verifiable fact. Opinions are not held out as verifiable statements of fact, a prerequisite for a libelous communication. Instead, responsible opinions rest on reliable information, facts from which different interpreters can reasonably arrive at varying conclusions. The First Amendment protects that independence of individual thought. But if an opinion rests on a factual falsehood instead of a verifiable fact, it might be considered defamatory.

Esquire's biting follow-up characterized the lies told by Corsi and Farah as "despicable"—deserving "only ridicule." Farah claimed the piece was not a disclaimer at all but rather a new defamatory publication. *Esquire* in turn argued that the second article subjectively explained the earlier column and was not offered for its truth. The appeals court ruled that the disclaimer, with its negative characterization of the statements as despicable, was an opinion, outside the definition of defamation, and protected by the First Amendment.

The potential disputes between WND and Warren did not end there. In an interview with the right-wing website the Daily Caller on the day Warren's article appeared, Warren had referred to Corsi as "an 'execrable piece of shit.'" Those words too were clearly both hyperbole and opinion, protected by the First Amendment. Warren's characterization of Corsi was, the court said, "the sort of loose, figurative or hyperbolic language" that signals it should not be taken literally. All sorts of rude and crude names and labels meeting that description are treated as opinion, not statements of fact susceptible to proof.[18]

Lessons of *Farah v. Esquire*

Consideration of Farah and Corsi's meritless defamation claim illustrates three principles.

First, when communications are simply not credible, it is not reasonable to conclude that the speaker intended to deceive. Satirists and other over-the-top speakers acknowledge that they are transmitting falsehoods and simultaneously signal that they do not expect any listener to believe something so patently false as to be literally incredible.

The second principle is closely related to the first: No harm is possible when the speaker has not offered any credible statements of fact. If the falsehoods are too incredible for a reasonable person to believe them, then as far as the law is concerned the statement cannot damage anyone's reputation. Beyond satire, this principle also explains why it would be unreasonable to treat an opinion as defamatory. Opinions cannot cause legally recognizable harm because they do not purport to offer verifiable facts, though speakers may share the facts that led to their opinions.

Those two principles gained rare public recognition in 2021, when attorneys for former Trump lawyer Sidney Powell disingenuously relied on them. Powell had been sued for defamation based on allegedly false statements she made while seeking to overturn the 2020 presidential election results. It is a misuse of the "too incredible to be believed" defense to peddle fiction as truth and then, in the face of a defamation suit, to retrospectively claim that "no reasonable person would conclude that the statements were truly statements of fact." This is exactly what Powell argued when she asked a federal court to dismiss the defamation case against her.

After the 2020 election, Powell called on courts and citizens to "Stop the Steal."

She charged that the 2020 election result was "the greatest crime of the century if not the life of the world." Her public falsehoods supported an active litigation strategy in which she stopped short of making false claims of fraud and the like in her court filings. Because attorneys can lose their licenses to practice law for lying to a court, the pronounced silence in Powell's court papers suggests that she knew her public statements were not true. Powell's out-of-court statements did not carry any suggestion that she was joking, engaging in hyperbole, or merely voicing an opinion—all defenses her lawyers later offered when they asked the court to dismiss the defamation suit. They also argued that her statements were political and thus inherently unreliable.

But the same motion papers in which Powell's attorneys claimed that her statements (for example, that a deceased Venezuelan dictator plotted to rig voting machines that would be used to subvert a US election years after he died) were too "outlandish" to be believed, simultaneously asserted that Powell "believed the allegations then and she believes them now."[19]

One cannot have it both ways. The incredibility defense is not infinitely elastic. Speakers must decide early on whether they intend others to believe their words are factual. In contrast to Powell's initial statements, which lacked signals that her words were not to be taken seriously, her purportedly serious motion to dismiss (still pending as I write) seems risible.

The third principle drawn from *Farah*: responsibility for sorting truth from falsehood is divided between the speaker and the listeners. Before a speaker may be held accountable for a defamatory utterance, it must be shown that a reasonable recipient of the falsehood could reasonably believe that the statement conveyed the truth about actual facts. The test assumes that the reasonable listener has the capacity to exercise well-informed common sense. Defamation doctrine acknowledges with an implied shrug that some listeners may be misled. That's on them, even if the subject of the falsehood suffers. In the judicial balancing, the regime of free speech requires readers and listeners to learn to be more discerning so that robust protected speech is not needlessly inhibited.

Sometimes, listeners prove up to the task. In 2020, Trump's supporters failed in their effort to derail another person of color—Democratic vice presidential candidate Kamala Harris—with another birtherism hoax. This time, they asserted that Harris was not a citizen despite having been born in the United States, because her parents were here as university students. If that radical proposition had been accepted it would have stripped unknown numbers of children born in the United States of citizenship. Fortunately, almost no one appears to have taken the bait, and the Harris birtherism attack quickly faded away, at least in mainstream media.

Birtherism II: The Hypothetical Case of *Obama* v. *Corsi*

Now, I invite you to engage in a classical law school thought experiment. Let's consider the birtherism controversy through the lens of a different lawsuit that could have been pursued but never happened.

A reasonable reader of this book may well wonder why Corsi and Farah were the ones seeking recompense for having been defamed when if anyone was defamed during the events leading up to and surrounding the publication of *Where's the Birth Certificate?* it was President Obama. Why, one might ask, didn't Obama sue the authors and publishers?

At first glance, the facts would appear to satisfy all four elements of a successful defamation claim. Birtherism asserts a demonstrably false fact—Obama was not born in the United States—that when put out to the public damaged Obama's reputation and professional standing by proclaiming his ineligibility for the presidency and accusing him of presenting forged birth documents to the public. Corsi, Farah, and other birthers intended to harm Obama; their allegations were at least reckless if not intentionally dishonest. And they indisputably damaged Obama's reputation among those who fell for the deceit. Many people apparently thought Obama ineligible for the presidency; they spurned the birth certificates he presented to prove his birthplace. It would seem that "more and better speech" failed to correct the record, making damages appropriate.

And yet, Obama had been elected, sworn in, and was serving as president. Did that mean he had not actually been damaged?

Perhaps the people who took birtherism seriously were simply not reasonable in light of the evidence, including the birth certificates that the president had posted on the web and that mainstream media had covered intensely.

Consider the alternative possibility that respondents who told pollsters they believed the birtherism conspiracy was true actually *knew* that Corsi, Farah, Trump, Fox News hosts, and the like were just trying to rile them up, giving them an excuse to pile on to a politician they hated for other reasons. For them, birtherism might have been just another example of posturing or political performance rather than a serious allegation. The birther crowd might have thought the whole brouhaha hilarious. In that event, Obama would not have been harmed in the legal sense.

We shall never know.

But there is a second, completely contradictory way to escape a finding of intent. It might have been difficult for Obama as a plaintiff in a defamation suit to show that the speakers intended to deceive because birtherism's proponents may have actually believed their fantasies. They may have been impervious to contradictory evidence.

Some speakers believe that they speak the truth even if no one else does. In the case of climate change or vaccinations, they may not understand or may reject scientific methods and findings. They may be completely delusional. Any of these circumstances prevents a court from finding that a speaker intended to deceive others.

If Corsi, Farah, or Trump *actually* believed that Obama had not been born in Hawaii and that he presented forged documents to prove otherwise, and none of them credited the possibility that they could be mistaken, the hypothetical Obama who could have pursued any of the three for defamation might not have been able to prove the crucial element of actual malice. If they entertained no doubts, then arguably they were not sufficiently reckless to meet the actual malice test. It could be legally irrelevant that the factual falsehoods they were spreading lacked any basis in reality.

While the little known average person must only establish that the speaker who got it wrong was negligent, or careless, recall that in *Sullivan* the Supreme Court imposed a higher standard—actual malice—when public figures bring defamation suits, and today the class of public figures reaches far beyond those who hold public office to many sorts of celebrities. Public figures who have chosen to stand out sacrifice some of the privacy others normally expect—or at least that regular folks were entitled to expect before the social media age, when they routinely exchange privacy for access. Kim Kardashian offers a prime example. Her whole life is devoted to public exposure for what appears to be its own sake. Obama and Jerry Falwell, the latter of whose unsuccessful suit against *Hustler* was discussed above, were also public figures.

Public figures must prove the speaker's actual malice to win a defamation case, but actual malice does not mean what the words commonly suggest. As a legal standard, it means that the speaker had reason to think the statement might be false and published it anyway or proceeded with reckless disregard of the truth. These elements are exceedingly difficult to prove, and intentionally so. In addition, a public figure must meet a higher burden of proof, meaning that person must prove the case by clear and convincing evidence, higher than the "preponderance of the evidence" that juries must find in civil cases between private parties, though not as high as the "beyond a reasonable doubt" standard used in criminal trials. These elevated requirements are designed to protect wide-ranging public debate, however nasty it might get, by erecting hurdles to success in defamation cases brought by public figures, especially when the subject matter is of public interest.

Since we are engaged in fantasy here, if President Obama had consulted me about whether to sue those spreading birtherism falsehoods, I would have advised him not to pursue his claim, even if I thought he might win despite being a public figure. A trial would only give Corsi, Trump, and the rest an even bigger media platform over countless news cycles for broadcasting their lies about him, and expose him to the costs, burden, and disclosure of personal details that would accompany pretrial discovery. Small wonder a reportedly frustrated, bemused, and sometimes amused President Obama declined to be drawn into litigation over birtherism. To sue would give the allegations more credit than they deserved.

Joe Scarborough Murdered a Staff Member

Here is another problem ripe for discussion in a law school class: a dispute that actually occurred between President Trump and Joe Scarborough, a former Republican and former congressman turned successful MSNBC morning news host who regularly took President Trump to task. The dispute implicated potential defamation claims but never led to a lawsuit. The facts expose additional facets of defamation doctrine: slippery rhetoric may protect a defamer, and some real victims cannot avail themselves of the legal remedy.

In the spring of 2020 Trump tweeted his baseless view that in 2001 Scarborough had murdered Lori Klausutis, a young woman who had worked in his congressional office. In a series of tweets in March Trump speculated:

> Did he get away with murder? Some people think so. Keep digging . . . So a young marathon runner just happened to faint in his office, hit her head on his desk, & die? I would think there is a lot more to this story than that? An affair? . . .

... I find Joe to be a total Nut Job, and I knew him well, far
better than most. So many unanswered & obvious questions, but I
won't bring them up now! Law enforcement eventually will?[20]

Trump also speculated that Scarborough had declined to seek reelection
and fled Congress to avoid closer scrutiny of the murder.

Those insinuations and accusations were entirely untethered from the
facts. Scarborough was in Washington, D.C., when twenty-eight-year-old
Klausutis fell in his Florida office, struck her head on a desk, and died. The
police found no evidence of a crime. An autopsy concluded that Klausutis
had an undiagnosed heart condition that led her to faint; falling, she hit her
head on the desk. The resulting injury caused her death. Yet President
Trump screamed cover-up nineteen years later. He emphasized that there
was no statute of limitations for murder and demanded a renewed
investigation.

Trump cleverly used rhetorical devices to distance himself from appear-
ing to state facts. He postured: I don't necessarily think this happened, but
"some people" do. Instead of using declarative sentences, Trump asked
questions: "An affair?" Innuendo runs through these and other tweets.
Trump promises not to bring up the "many unanswered & obvious questions," implying they are too numerous to list.

When reporters asked President Trump about the "false accusation" in
the Rose Garden, he "doubled down," according to the *New York Times*, using similar ways of avoiding responsibility: "A lot of people suggest that....
It's certainly a very suspicious situation. Very sad, very sad and very suspicious." Reporters accurately labeled Trump's tweets and public statements
"wild allegations and fact-free innuendo."[21]

Innuendo may imply that the speaker knows facts that are not yet available to the audience. However, if the speaker implies knowledge of additional facts that could either be verified or shown to be false, innuendo will
not shelter the implicit statement of fact from accountability as defamation.
Here, Trump asserted that he knew Scarborough "well, far better than
most," and that he had concluded based on that knowledge that Scarborough was a "Nut Job." A reasonable person perusing Trump's tweets could
be expected to assume that the president knew things about Scarborough's
mental state the rest of us did not. This opened a crack in Trump's potential
defense that he was only opining; his opinion appeared to rest on implied
verifiable facts.

Who did President Trump's accusations harm? Clearly Scarborough, if anyone believed the charges. But he did not pursue a libel claim against the sitting president. Very likely the considerations that would have inhibited President Obama from suing his defamers contributed to Scarborough's decision. He has also publicly discussed the legal barriers to suing the social media sites that hosted Trump's comments and facilitated their rapid spread, which federal law protects from liability for speech by those who use the sites. And it would be impractical to try to sue the many Trump followers who retweeted his false accusations.

Scarborough was not the only victim of Trump's cruelty. The accusations also devastated Lori's survivors, whom the law views as mere bystanders to any defamation claim.

Trump did not accuse the survivors of any disgraceful attributes or acts. Timothy Klausutis, Lori's widower, begged Twitter to remove the president's posts, which caused her family "such deep pain" nineteen years after her death. Timothy wrote to Jack Dorsey, Twitter's CEO: "As her husband, I feel that one of my marital obligations is to protect her memory as I would have protected her in life." Scarborough, along with his cohost and spouse, Mika Brzezinski, also demanded that Twitter remove the president's tweets about Klausutis. Twitter refused.

Defamation law does not offer any remedy to Timothy Klausutis. Trump did not say anything at all about Timothy, much less anything that could reasonably be construed as damaging his reputation, with the possible exception of alleging that his deceased wife might have had an extramarital affair. Trump did not directly call Timothy a cuckold, but even if he had, that might not have been construed as damaging to Timothy's reputation in 2020. Lori's survivors suffered, but the law does not compensate for emotional trauma caused by speech. The First Amendment generally bars punishment for speech that hurts feelings, even in the context of defamatory falsehoods.

Under completely different hypothetical circumstances, Lori might have had a claim against Trump. Saying Lori had an extramarital affair with her boss might have damaged Lori's reputation, even in the twenty-first century, if Lori had been alive. But she was dead, and there is no defamation remedy for the deceased.

Scarborough attributed the attack to his frequent criticisms of the president. Instigating criminal investigations of media critics to distract from policy failures like the raging COVID-19 pandemic and a collapsing economy, Scarborough charged, is "what Putin does. That's what Orban does. That's what autocrats have been doing for centuries." Timothy Klausutis seemed to agree when he told Dorsey that the president had "perverted" the "memory of my dead wife" for "political gain."[22]

Defamation Law in the Public Square

Obama and Timothy Klausutis are not the only victims of defamation who lack a legal remedy in the face of scurrilous falsehoods: the American people are victimized by fictions like birtherism. Baseless fantasies and conspiracy theories skew political discussion, distract from genuine policy choices, and undermine meaningful voter participation—just as the conspiracy proponents intend.

Paradoxically, some serial defamers like Corsi and Trump use defamation law to attack their critics. They pervert the doctrine to pose as victims.

In addition to suing Warren and *Esquire*, Corsi has perversely sued others who he claims have defamed or harmed him. In the last few years alone, he sued Roger Stone and, separately, Infowars founder Alex Jones for defamation. He also sued Robert Mueller (whose redacted 2019 *Special Counsel's Report* mentions Corsi multiple times) for alleged prosecutorial misconduct.

Like Corsi, Trump hides behind defamation law's nuances when he is the defamer, and then, when he is the target of criticism, weaponizes defamation in an effort to stifle responsible journalism. Early in 2020, for example, he filed a series of lawsuits alleging that the *New York Times*, the *Washington Post*, and CNN had all defamed him. In each instance, Trump objected to an opinion piece about Russian influence on him.[23] And, in each instance, factual corroboration for the opinions is easily found: in the Mueller Report, in quotes from Trump himself, and in his refusal to take any steps to prevent foreign interference in the 2020 election.

Wrongful weaponization of defamation law by accomplished defamers turns libel law on its head. In the United States, defamation law aims to promote speech, not to muzzle it, even at the risk that some lies will gain traction. A legal doctrine crafted to discourage the powerful from attacking the innocent is too often misused in an effort to shelter liars from accountability and enable the powerful to silence their critics. So far, the courts have generally not let them get away with it. The risk remains that speakers who lack the resources of a CNN will shy away from speech that might provoke a libel suit.

Responding to such abuses, many states have passed statutes to prevent intimidation known as anti-SLAPP (strategic lawsuits against public participation) laws. These laws allow rapid dismissal of lawsuits that aim to silence speech about matters of public concern.

Nefarious speakers sometimes wrongly invoke anti-SLAPP provisions seeking protections for factual falsehoods that pollute political debate. In early 2021, for instance, the highest court in Texas ruled that its anti-SLAPP law did not protect conspiracy theorist Alex Jones and his site Infowars from lawsuits filed by families of children who had been killed in the Sandy Hook school shooting. Jones had preposterously charged that the government had faked the shootings and that the families who appeared in public were actually actors who helped with the cover-up.[24]

Despite the potential for abuse, used as intended defamation law serves critical First Amendment goals by combating disinformation. Shortly before this book went to press, voting technology providers Dominion and Smartmatic filed a spate of lawsuits that charged individuals and media outlets with defamation for falsely implicating them in unsubstantiated efforts to steal the 2020 election from Donald Trump. The defendants include Sidney Powell (whose motion to dismiss I discussed above), Rudolph Giuliani, and other attorneys who represented Trump, as well as Fox News, and named Fox reporters, including Lou Dobbs, a former Fox personality, now sidelined in the wake of the lawsuit against him. Those lawsuits help us to understand how defamation law promotes First Amendment purposes.

Dominion, whose technology was used by more than 40 percent of all voters, filed detailed complaints with exhibits that link the alleged defamatory lies to, in the company's words, "a false preconceived narrative about the 2020 election." Dominion's complaints allege that the various defendants accused it of serious criminal acts, damaged its core business, and gave rise to credible death threats against its employees. The falsehoods also threatened democracy, Dominion charges, by attempting to delegitimize elections and contributing to the violent January 6 uprising.[25]

In a similar vein, a lawyer for the "never-Trump" Lincoln Project (led by former Republican strategists) excoriated Guiliani's false allegation that the Project had "planned" the seditious January 6 insurrection. Demanding an immediate retraction at the risk of an imminent lawsuit, the Project's attorney wrote: "You committed a textbook act of defamation. You publicly accused the Lincoln Project of an infamous and criminal act that it had nothing to do with, as you well know. You lied."[26]

That lawyer is right. Those facts, if proven, present a textbook example of classic defamation. If this were a law school class on basic doctrine, I might have opened with it.

In its more complex forms, US defamation law serves freedom of expression in two seemingly contradictory ways that provide remarkable coherence. It limits the scope of defamation claims to promote the public debate vital to our democracy, while it provides a legal remedy for knowing falsehoods that infect public discourse.

PART III

Lies Affecting Democracy

CHAPTER 4

The Ministry of Truth:
Uncontrollable Campaign Lies

The founders and the Supreme Court justices who crafted modern Speech Clause doctrine were confident that truth would prevail in robust political debate. What if it does not?

The distinction between truth and falsehood in politics has been at the center of a national maelstrom for years, especially since the 2016 election season. Candidates and officeholders are fact-checked, awarded Pinocchios, and sometimes indicted, for half-truths, untruths, and fantastical fabrications.

After the 2016 election cycle, the Pulitzer Prize–winning PolitiFact awarded its 2015 annual distinction "Lie of the Year" to the collective "campaign misstatements of Donald Trump," based on "inaccurate statistics and dubious accounts of his own record and words" that "exhibited range, boldness and a blatant disregard for the truth."[1] Nothing in modern history prior to 2016 had prepared American journalists, commentators, or voters for the rampant affirmative lies, false denials, and conspiratorial accusations of the two Trump campaigns.

Trump's propensity for contra-factual bombast continued during his term in office and accelerated during the 2020 election cycle. Commentators largely agreed that the 2020 Republican National Convention that nominated Trump for a second term consisted of a constant stream of outright falsehoods, including many in his acceptance speech:

- As to the pandemic killing one thousand people a day: "We are meeting this challenge. We are delivering lifesaving therapies." For weeks after that he insisted, we have "rounded the corner," even after he tested positive for COVID-19 on October 2;

- As to the economy, stating: "We have seen the smallest economic contraction of any major western nation, and we are recovering much faster," ignoring a record-breaking second quarter contraction in gross domestic product of 31.7 percent, and data showing smaller contractions in non-western industrialized South Korea and Japan and positive growth in China. At least 11.5 million more Americans were unemployed as he spoke than before the pandemic hit; and

- As to his opponent, falsely attributing positions to Joe Biden that Biden had expressly repudiated, saying this election will decide whether "we save the American Dream . . . or whether we give free rein to violent anarchists, agitators, and criminals who threaten our citizens . . . whether we will defend the American Way of Life, or whether we allow a radical movement to completely dismantle and destroy it."[2]

CNN's fact-checker Daniel Dale concluded that Trump was a "serial liar" at the convention. Five weeks later, after the first presidential debate, Dale lambasted Trump's debate performance in even more robust terms: "an avalanche of lying." Dale added, "Almost every single thing he said" in the last part "of the debate was inaccurate."[3]

Finally, as Trump ramped up his lies during the campaign to more than fifty a day, Dale metaphorically threw up his hands: "I had to abandon my 3.75-year count of every Trump false claim," he tweeted. "Because he's talking so much and telling so many important lies that I don't have the time to research all the little ones." The *Washington Post* fact-checkers agreed. They had stopped counting when Trump formally accepted the Republican nomination. They had already fallen eight weeks behind and were simply unable to keep up.[4]

The party faithful helped to spin the convention's false narrative of a world in which there was neither disease nor massive unemployment, and in which (contrary to his record in office and before) Trump championed persons of color while cheerfully granting immigrants citizenship, using them as props in a televised ceremony without their prior knowledge or consent. That ceremony may not have been a lie in the technical sense, but it surely was deceptive, both in its abuse of real people and its message, which flew in the face of Trump's pervasive anti-immigrant rhetoric and policy.

The week leading up to the 2020 Labor Day weekend witnessed an explosion of "doctored and misleading videos," known as "deep fakes," circulated by Trump and other Republicans. In one instance, the Trump campaign aired a video of Biden himself saying, "You won't be safe in Joe Biden's America." The video edited out the surrounding words, which made clear that Biden was incredulously asking whether anyone would believe Trump's preposterous allegations about what the future would hold under Biden: a socialist country without suburbs, overtaken by riots, with windowless skyscrapers.[5]

Another doctored video Trump tweeted on August 30, 2020, captioned "Black Lives Matter/Antifa," showed a Black man pushing a White woman on a subway platform. The Black man featured in the video did not belong to either of the captioned groups. The film had been shot in 2019, before the 2020 wave of Black Lives Matter protests that followed the death of George Floyd. And contrary to the ad's insinuations and Trump's repeated attacks, those 2020 protests were almost uniformly (93 percent) peaceful, according to an independent nonprofit group. The list of intentionally misleading ads that campaign season continues, including ads supporting two Republican Senate candidates, one of whom darkened the skin of his Black opponent (Jaime Harrison, whom Lindsey Graham defeated), while the other elongated the nose of his Jewish rival (current senator Jon Ossoff).[6]

Trump and his campaign insisted without any basis that Biden suffered from dementia, was feeble, and taking performance-enhancing drugs. Within days of the first presidential debate, Trump's team purchased ads on Facebook falsely claiming that Vice President Biden had received illegal prompts throughout the debate through an earpiece or something hidden in his jacket.

Michael Gableman, a county judge running to unseat a justice on the Wisconsin Supreme Court in 2008, also relied on a heavily misleading television advertisement. The video inaccurately conveyed the impression that his opponent bore responsibility for a horrendous crime committed by a former client whom he had represented in a criminal appeal.

The judges who considered the resulting judicial ethics charges against Gableman proved unable to agree about almost anything. Most critically, they were at loggerheads over whether the statements in the ad amounted to falsehoods. Gableman's story, which I share more fully later in this chapter, offers several cautionary tales about efforts to regulate campaign speech. Looking beyond the First Amendment hurdles, the *Gableman* case reveals how the many ways of conveying falsehoods create barriers to achieving the very first step toward regulation—consensus about what utterances count as lies.

Judge Gableman's commercial was reminiscent of one of the most notorious advertisements in US history: the "Willie Horton" ad. In 1988, then-Republican candidate George H. W. Bush benefited from a television commercial featuring Willie Horton, a convicted murderer who failed to return to a Massachusetts prison after a standard weekend furlough. The next year in Maryland, Horton stabbed a man and raped the man's fiancée in their home. Known as the "Weekend Passes" ad, the video blamed Michael Dukakis, the Democratic candidate for president and sitting governor of Massachusetts, for releasing Horton from prison, an act deemed to have led directly to the assault and rape in Maryland. The ad branded Dukakis as soft on crime and, combined with Dukakis's inability to craft a strong response, essentially eviscerated his campaign. And the candidate was able to deny any responsibility for the ad because third parties who supported Bush had created and distributed it. The ad proved so effective that it has become a verb: candidates fear being "Willie Hortoned."

The Willie Horton ad was profoundly misleading, although each fact taken in isolation might be viewed as "true." The furlough program had been in place since 1972, before Dukakis became governor. The federal government and nearly all states had prison furlough programs at the time; at least sixteen states offered extended furloughs to prisoners who had been convicted of first degree murder. Dukakis had no personal involvement with Horton's weekend leave or anything that happened afterward. When the ad ran, Horton was already safely behind bars again.

Varieties of Falsehood

One reason so many people believe politicians always lie is the wide range of falsehoods beyond the bald-faced lies that come into play during electoral campaigns at every level of government. The varieties of effective campaign falsehoods that have attracted reform efforts require me to press beyond verifiable factual falsehoods.

Intentional distortion—a statement resting on verifiable facts that creates a misleading narrative—is one of the most prominent deceptive rhetorical postures in political campaigns. Such distortions sometimes involve false claims of credit for popular programs. For instance, according to CNN, Trump knowingly distorted his record with respect to the successful Veteran's Choice Program some 150 times before the first 2020 presidential debate. He claimed full credit for the program, which primarily allows veterans to see private physicians when the waiting time at Veterans Administration medical facilities is too long. However, President Obama signed the Veterans' Choice Program into law. It was merely revised and expanded during Trump's term.

Another form of intentional distortion misleads by using facts out of context. The problem is evidenced in the misuse of votes on omnibus legislation to attack candidates by tarring them with positions they never endorsed. Omnibus legislation describes the increasingly common practice of piling all sorts of unrelated measures into one bill that is likely to pass because it includes urgent measures that few people want to vote against. It enables distortion by facilitating willful failure to disaggregate multiple issues that have been artificially compacted in the bill. For instance, a candidate who opposes so-called pork might nonetheless vote to approve the annual budget, even though it is filled with lard, and then be accused of voting for pork-barrel spending. Similarly, an incumbent who vociferously opposes abortion may be accused of supporting "taxpayer-funded abortion" because she voted for a broad health insurance bill that incidentally provided abortion funding. Because there is a sliver of factual basis for these intentional distortions, they are not readily labeled as verifiable factual falsehoods, are hard to pin down, and appear to escape regulation.

Prevarication, a statement that while not strictly false can be read in different ways, is another common form of falsehood. It is comparable to an opinion that cannot lead to liability under defamation law because it cannot be proved or disproved. It is joined by indirect prevarication, which is framed so that the speaker escapes responsibility. Trump's use of "some people think" in accusing Joe Scarborough of murder exemplifies indirect prevarication.

Other forms of indirectness defy classification, as in an oft-repeated story about the young Lyndon Baines Johnson running for Congress that may well be apocryphal. Johnson is reputed to have asked his campaign manager to circulate the story that his opponent was a "pig-fucker." The manager, clearly fearing a libel suit, warned Johnson, "You can't prove he's a pig-fucker." To which Johnson replied, "I don't have to prove it, I just have to catch him denying it."

As I showed in discussing defamation, numerous rhetorical forms allow the speaker to avoid legal responsibility because no one should believe they offer verifiable facts. These include opinion, hyperbole, and satire. They are joined by "bullshit," famously analyzed by philosopher Harry Frankfurt. Speakers are bullshitting when they do not know or, more importantly, do not care if what they say is true.[7] The content conveyed by any of these devices is not offered as factual truth.

Similarly, campaign promises that go unfulfilled should not be regarded as lies because they are at best mere intentions. Many intervening events outside the candidate's control—like insufficient support in the legislature or budget shortfalls—may stand in the way of fulfilling the promise, even if the candidate fully intends to carry through. Equally important, a promise that something will happen in the future resembles a prediction: it does not state a fact we can verify today. A campaign promise may be slightly more concrete than a fortune-teller's prediction that "you will meet a dark, handsome man," but one can no more rely on it than my law students should bank on my educated reassurance that they will pass the bar exam.

In the face of an increasing disconnect between verifiable facts and political discourse, a lack of embarrassment about outright fabrication, and a divide between voters who appear to be operating based on completely different sets of "facts," it is reasonable to ask why our society allows such pervasive falsehoods affecting our most critical shared decision making to flourish without restraint. Halfway through this volume the legal answer should not surprise anyone: the Speech Clause poses a virtually insurmountable obstacle to efforts to regulate deceptive campaign speech by candidates and their supporters.

And that is all to the good. Robust public debate tests our commitment to free expression, but the alternative would be rampant government censorship.

Regulatory Regimes

As of 2018, at least sixteen states had laws in place aimed at lies told by candidates and their supporters during campaigns for elective office. Since the Supreme Court held in 2012 that the Speech Clause extends to falsehoods, not a single campaign deception statute has survived a First Amendment challenge outside the highly specialized context of judicial elections. Deception in judicial elections is governed by ethical codes that apply only to judges and candidates for judicial office and is treated as a matter of professional self-policing—not state censorship. I will return to judicial elections below.

The Supreme Court has underscored that accusatory stabs at opponents are the very stuff of electoral contests: the "clash of reputations is the staple of election campaigns." Explaining why defamation law would be inappropriate in the context of campaigns, the Supreme Court noted that voters want to know everything they can about candidates: "It is by no means easy to see what statements about a candidate might be altogether without relevance to his fitness for the office he seeks."[8] The Biden campaign's slogan "Truth over lies" gained salience as an express comparison of the candidates' characters.

State legislators trying to rein in campaign deception often modeled regulations on defamation law. Some states, like Florida, require that the speaker proceeded with "actual malice" when making false statements of fact. Mississippi too tracks defamation law very closely, penalizing charges about the "honesty, integrity, or moral character of any candidate, so far as his or her private life is concerned, unless the charge be in fact true and actually capable of proof." The statute treats any statements that "clearly and unmistakably imply" attacks on personal integrity as violations.[9] That language would reach both bald-faced lies about opponents and intentional distortions about an opponent's character. Courts have repeatedly overturned state regulations that failed to integrate First Amendment limitations on libel suits into campaign deception laws.

Some of the false allegations that candidates lob at opponents are clearly defamatory if untrue: "he's a crook" or "he defrauded the elderly." At first glance, it might seem that a candidate maligned by her opponent through a bald-faced falsehood might seek relief by suing for defamation. However, all candidates for office are public figures no matter how small the pond in which they stand for election. As a consequence, to prevail a candidate would need to show the speaker's actual malice or reckless disregard for truth, hard standards to meet.[10]

In the unlikely scenario that a public figure prevailed in a defamation suit based on a campaign falsehood, resolution of the dispute would likely come after the election is in a distant rearview mirror. Exacerbating the inability of the legal process to keep up with the harm, campaign falsehoods commonly gain steam shortly before voting takes place. The short time frame until Election Day makes it much more difficult for the candidate who was besmirched to respond effectively in public debate or with counter-advertising.

The lie's timing does not affect its legal treatment. The lie is out there, and given the notorious persistence of misinformation, might be very difficult to dislodge under the best of circumstances, where there is unlimited time and budget to spread the repetition of the truth.

But elections have a deadline. The lie is in play. This is the very evil the regulations are intended to redress.

An unintended but easily predictable consequence flows from the regulatory scheme. The target of the alleged lie may weaponize the regulatory apparatus to smear an innocent opponent. The allegation, initiating an investigation, is reported in the press, tarnishing the original speaker, who may not have been lying at all. A dismissal of charges will not come until many months after the election is over.

Broadly, the state regulations on campaign speech that remain in place in 2021 would reach a wide variety of falsehoods if enforceable. They take a number of common approaches beyond reliance on defamation doctrine.

A few jurisdictions prohibit deceptive speech only to the extent that it tends to benefit the candidate or a candidate with whom the speaker is associated. These include bald-faced biographical lies about themselves during a campaign, such as falsely claiming a Congressional Medal of Honor or that they received an endorsement they did not have, as Trump did during the first debate of 2020 when he wrongly announced that the Portland, Oregon sheriff had endorsed him. Multnomah County sheriff Mike Reese quickly repudiated Trump, tweeting, "I have never supported Donald Trump and will never support him."[11] We assume knowledge of falsehood because the candidate knows better than anyone whether misleading biographical information is true or false. Words, facts, and specifics matter.

Statutes that target false speech about an opponent sometimes assert power to reach beyond bald-faced lies. Those laws include clauses like "any statement about an opposing candidate which is false."[12] *Any* statement? Consider the candidate who recounts a story about a meeting with an opponent: "When we met for a drink at nine, she was wearing a blue suit." But the details are false; they met at eight, and she was dressed in red. If asserted as truth and spoken about an opponent, all of the details that turn out to be false could be swept up in the statute's plain language. The discrepancies may be pertinent to challenging a trial witness's memory but should not be viewed as likely to affect voters' decisions. The time and outfit are unlikely to cut to the gist of the story's message.

A handful of states outlaw falsehoods in specific settings, such as polling places (where many states outlaw all electioneering), and during telephone polling. Telephone polling is notorious for "push-polling," where pollsters ask questions in the form "Would it change your opinion if . . ." or "Did you know . . ." without claiming that the assertions following those words are true. In the 2000 Republican primary in South Carolina, for example, push-pollers intimated that John McCain had "fathered an illegitimate black child."[13]

Strictly Scrutinizing Campaign Lies

Those state statutes present a constitutional question: Is it possible for any laws outlawing deception in political campaigns to survive First Amendment scrutiny? Or do such laws raise the specter of George Orwell's Ministry of Truth?

The Ministry of Truth wielded enormous power in the Oceania of Orwell's *1984*. Like other ministries in Oceania, it does the opposite of what its name suggests. The Ministry of Truth is actually the Ministry of Lies. That is, it falsifies the past and the present, ensuring no other sources of information are available for public consumption, so that whatever the rulers declare as true becomes "truth." It is the perfect propaganda machinery for the state because it methodically eliminates all sources of conflicting ideas and messages even as it scales back language itself. Oceania's Newspeak makes heretical thought literally "unthinkable" by systematically eliminating words like "justice" and "democracy" so that the concepts those words capture "simply ceased to exist."[14]

In contrast to dystopias and authoritarian regimes, the Speech Clause forbids any "broad censorial power" vested in government. Recall that "as a general matter, the First Amendment means that government has no power to restrict expression because of its message, its ideas, its subject matter, or its content."[15] Any effort to proscribe a bald-faced lie or an indirect prevarication or anything in between on account of its falsehood necessarily rests on its content. The Supreme Court has pointedly told us that "our constitutional tradition" has no place for Orwell's "Ministry of Truth." Justices of every political stripe agree: "It is perilous to permit the state to be the arbiter of truth."[16]

Commentators before and after *Alvarez* have disagreed about whether *any* effort to restrain deception during political campaigns could withstand First Amendment challenge. Some think the First Amendment bars all regulation of campaign speech, while other authorities have argued that the unique dangers inherent in false manipulation of voters should outweigh free speech concerns. Still others, like Diogenes seeking the honest person, are on a quest to craft a statute that would strike the right balance between freedom of expression and electoral integrity.

The state places a content-based thumb on the marketplace of ideas when it constrains campaign expression. If the mere imposition of regulations did not violate the Speech Clause, administering and enforcing them surely would, because campaign speech regulations rely on the government to discern what is true or false.

Statutes and regulations purporting to inhibit deceptive campaign speech rely on one of two approaches to enforcement. In one scenario, candidates or concerned citizens may file complaints in court. Alternatively, they may ask a state agency or prosecutor to determine whether it appears that a campaign engaged in the type of deceptive speech the statute bars, and if so, demand that the case be referred for further proceedings. In either instance, the state (whether through the executive branch, an independent agency, or the judiciary) becomes the arbiter of truth.

As the Supreme Court explained in *New York Times* v. *Sullivan*, the precise method the government uses to impose truthfulness is irrelevant: "Authoritative interpretations of the First Amendment guarantees have consistently refused to recognize an exception for any test of truth—whether administered by judges, juries, or administrative officials."[17]

The constitutional bar on governmental tests of truth suffices to end the analysis. But a closer look indicates that campaign falsehood regulations would not survive constitutional review for other reasons as well.

We have, the Supreme Court reminds us again and again, "a profound national commitment to the principle that debate on public issues should be uninhibited, robust and wide-open," including when candidates discuss government and politics.[18] The court has long warned that the breathing space the First Amendment requires for robust debate carries the risk of falsehoods and broken promises.

Political expression, especially speech related to political campaigns, is particularly sacrosanct. The foundational principle that content-based restrictions on expression are presumptively invalid has, the Supreme Court has stated, "'its fullest and most urgent application' to speech uttered during a campaign for political office."[19]

The reasons for protecting the flow of campaign messages are manifold, including the voters' need for information. As James Madison explained in 1800, electing public officials is "the essence of a free and responsible government. The value and efficacy of this right depends on the knowledge of the comparative merits and demerits of the candidates for public trust, and on the equal freedom, consequently, of examining and discussing these merits and demerits."[20]

In addition, campaign falsehood regulations might inadvertently distort political discourse because of the risk of selective prosecution. It is easy to imagine an administrative body with authority over campaign falsehood whose members were appointed by an incumbent governor who is running for reelection selectively choosing which deceptions merit investigation and which statements meet the definition of falsehood. Much less would be needed to find selective prosecution.

The US Courts of Appeals that have considered regulations on campaign speech since the Supreme Court decided *Alvarez* have all agreed that strict scrutiny must be used to assess the constitutionality of restrictions on electoral speech, even if a lesser standard might apply to falsehoods in other contexts. To survive strict scrutiny analysis, statutes and regulations that prohibit deception during electoral campaigns would need to show that a compelling interest necessitates the ban, that the ban resolves the problem, and that it does not abridge more speech than is necessary to accomplish its compelling goal. All of the campaign deception statutes that have reached the courts since 2012 have failed to satisfy that analysis and have been overturned.

The lower courts have had little difficulty finding that states have a compelling interest in regulating campaign lies, relying on the Supreme Court's summary of that interest: to preserve the integrity of the electoral process; to protect "voters from confusion and undue influence" caused by distortion and prevarication; and to ensure "that an individual's right to vote is not undermined by fraud in the election process."[21]

However, states overstep when they offer what the Massachusetts Supreme Judicial Court terms "the rather remarkable argument that the election context gives the government broader authority to restrict speech" in order to help citizens discern reliable campaign statements. The state's paternalistic argument seems to be that it should be allowed to eliminate confusing background noise. To the contrary, the highest court in Massachusetts held, a long line of cases make clear that "the opposite is true."[22] As the US Supreme Court has held, a state may not seek to enhance "the ability of its citizenry to make wise decisions by *restricting* the flow of information to them" (emphasis added).[23] Cutting off the flow of information violates voters' First Amendment right to receive information.

All the noise gets to come in when elections are at stake.

Another way of thinking about the state's compelling interest would be to ask whether the state was targeting the kinds of harms—the "something more" than even a flat-out factual falsehood—that the *Alvarez* plurality said were required before the state may constitutionally silence protected speech: harm to others or unwarranted advantage to the speaker. This inquiry turns out not to be simple either.

Presumably winning an election might be construed as securing employment or other benefit. For example, one might think that if Xavier Alvarez had falsely claimed to be a war hero during his election campaign instead of after he had won, and that claim had garnered votes for him, he would have obtained a concrete benefit. The highest court in Massachusetts considered and rejected that exact hypothetical argument. It concluded that a candidate who might make Alvarez's false claim "at a preelection debate" is constitutionally inoculated from criminal prosecution.[24]

No court appears to have asked whether misleading the public constitutes the sort of harm to others that could justify punishing liars, which itself suggests the answer is no. The harm contemplated by Justices Kennedy and Breyer in *Alvarez* appears to require an individual who suffers directly as a result of deceptive speech to establish that the falsehood already falls within the existing exceptions to the Speech Clause.

Establishing a compelling interest is just the beginning of the analysis. The state must next show that its regulations have a relationship to the danger it seeks to forestall, that the remedy is narrowly crafted so that it neither reaches too much speech (known as being overbroad) or too little speech to solve the problem (known as being underinclusive).

A tight "fit" or nexus is required between the compelling interest a regulation on speech is designed to serve and the specific inhibition on expression. The restriction must be "actually necessary" to achieve the state's goals, and the state must demonstrate "a direct causal link between the restriction imposed and the injury to be prevented."[25]

Government lawyers defending deceptive campaign speech statutes have asked courts to rely on common sense and conjecture about the likely impact of campaign lies. However, a reasonable inference is not a sufficient substitute for empirical evidence showing a close link between the harm to be prevented and the impact of suppressing protected speech. None of the reported cases contains evidence of the alleged harm. Failing that, the state cannot show that a verifiable harm creates a compelling interest in regulating campaign speech or that such regulations would ameliorate an established harm.

The secret ballot makes it very difficult to ascertain whether and to what extent voters were deceived by campaign falsehoods and whether they changed their votes as a result. The very proposition is undermined in cases where the victorious candidate is the one complaining that she was the target of the deceptive speech.

Many powerful forms of falsehood are beyond the reach of existing state and federal regulations on campaign speech, while other statutes unconstitutionally outlaw too much protected speech.

In order for the government's regulation of campaign deception to survive strict scrutiny, the regulatory scheme would need to address *all* (or at least a substantial amount) of the intentional deceit that was likely to undermine electoral integrity. At a minimum, a statute or regulatory rule would need to include all of the categories of lies I have set out: bald-faced lies about any candidate; intentional distortions that can be disproven; hyperbole that is too subtle to be immediately recognizable as not offering any believable facts; and prevarication, both direct and indirect—at least if it is shown to be knowing and intentional.

The existing campaign deception laws fall short of solving the problem when they target only bald-faced lies about opponents. They cannot promote the integrity of the electoral process if they fail to constrain the other kinds of lies to which candidates can pivot with great effect.[26]

Regulations also fail to reach other, rarer falsehoods. For example, candidates sometimes change their names. In one blatant instance, Scott Fistler ran in a Democratic primary in a heavily Hispanic Arizona district. He changed his name to Cesar Chavez despite having no discernible Latinx roots. Fistler apparently hoped to piggyback on the renown of the widely respected late labor organizer and civil rights activist whose reputation would presumably resonate with many of the district's voters. No state law stood in his way. When the Chavez family objected, the court dismissed their claim.[27]

Most, perhaps even all, of the existing campaign deception statutes are also underinclusive because they fail to address bald-faced factual falsehoods about substantive positions, such as the other candidate's platform, or either platform's likely costs and impact. During the 2020 presidential campaign, for example, President Trump and his spokespeople repeatedly lied about Joe Biden's positions on taxes, fracking, violence during political protests, and more. In mid-September Trump's campaign ran an ad accusing Biden of planning to use Social Security and Medicare funds to support illegal immigrants that displayed pictures of men climbing out of holes under a wall.

Throughout the 2020 campaign Trump also charged that, if elected president, Biden would remove protections that enable people with preexisting conditions to purchase health insurance. That assertion flew in the face of several realities. The Affordable Care Act, which became law during the Obama-Biden administration, protected people with preexisting conditions for the first time in US history. Trump not only pressed (unsuccessfully) for its repeal; his administration was challenging the act before the Supreme Court as Election Day loomed.

The only statutes that might reach this kind of bald-faced lie seem so overbroad in their reach as to be laughable. For example, Utah bars any false statement about either side that "is intended or tends to affect any voting at any primary, convention, or election." That definition reaches beyond candidates' false claims about themselves and their opponents (including Trump's misrepresentations about Biden's positions) to substantive ballot issues, such as referenda or constitutional amendments. Colorado's law also reaches substantive issues on the ballot. It forbids "any false statement designed to affect the vote on any issue submitted to the electors."[28]

The phrases "designed" and "tends to affect" reach a breathtakingly broad swath of falsehood. Why would a campaign say anything except to affect a vote? There are generally no guardrails around these provisions analogous to the actual malice or reckless disregard requirements for defamatory falsehoods about candidates.

States that regulate factual falsehoods about referenda and other ballot measures may confront another problem: bald-faced lies about substantive issues on the ballot may be beyond the law's reach because the lies target policies, not persons. In 1998 the Supreme Court of Washington held that the state lacked a compelling interest in regulating political advertisements that contained a false statement of material fact even if actual malice were shown—at least if the lies did not defame an actual person. The court expressly rejected the state's reliance on defamation law because the controversy involved a referendum; the absence of an individual whose private rights could be harmed or vindicated rendered defamation inapplicable. Where an initiative measure is involved, the court held, "there is no competing interest sufficient to override our precious freedom to vigorously debate the wisdom of enacting a measure, even if that debate contains falsehoods as well as truths."[29]

The ban on government censorship dooms efforts to craft better regulations. As the courts have explained, the claim that the state may "prohibit false statements of fact contained in political advertisements" or in a broader swath of expression "presupposes the State possesses an independent right to determine truth and falsity in political debate.... Rather, the First Amendment operates to insure [sic] the public decides what is true and false with respect to governance."[30]

Just What Is a Lie?
The Parable of Justice Michael Gableman, in Three Acts

Assuming that a regulation barring deceptive campaign speech survived a First Amendment challenge, it might still prove nearly impossible for regulators and judges to agree about what constitutes a lie. The problem does not entirely rest in postmodernist approaches to reality. It is at least partially traceable to a combination of definitional problems inherent in the variety of lies, pragmatic considerations including hyper-partisanship, and the remaining play in the joints of how the law defines truth and falsehood.

Nowhere are these dilemmas more apparent than in the drama surrounding Michael Gableman's election to the Supreme Court of Wisconsin in 2008. The saga illustrates the obstacles to reaching agreement about the baseline question of what constitutes a lie—a minimal precondition for reining in falsehood.

Forty-three states elected their judges as of 2020. They provide a sort of petri dish for testing the feasibility of identifying intentional and material falsehood. Almost all of them have judicial codes of ethics that restrict the speech of sitting judges and candidates for judicial office.

In stark contrast to regulations on campaign deception in other arenas, state judicial codes have largely survived First Amendment challenges. Everyone agrees that states have a compelling interest in preserving the integrity of the judicial system. Judicial codes of conduct, unlike statutes aimed at deception in campaigns for other offices, are often promulgated by the state's highest court and enforced as a matter of professional ethics and discipline.

Sitting judges are subject to a variety of rules that limit their expression in order to maintain the nonpartisanship and independence of the judiciary, or at least the appearance of independence. Under those rules, judges seeking reelection are uniquely prohibited from responding robustly to falsehoods about themselves or their records, rendering the usual First Amendment admonition to respond with more and better speech largely inapplicable.

The Supreme Court in *Republican Party of Minnesota* v. *White* held in 2002 that candidates for judicial office have speech rights; they cannot be prevented from sharing their views on unresolved legal questions. In a later case, however, the court upheld limits on direct fundraising by judicial candidates, rejecting a First Amendment challenge. Chief Justice Roberts, writing for the court in 2015, explained in *Williams-Yulee* v. *Florida Bar* that regulations on judicial campaign speech to preserve the courts' integrity and appearance of neutrality are justified because the "role of judges differs from the role of politicians."[31]

Gableman, Act One

Michael Gableman was a lowly administrative judge in Appleton, Wisconsin, when the Republican governor, Scott McCallum, snatched him from obscurity in 2002 to appoint him as the Burnett County circuit court judge.

In 2008, Gableman challenged sitting Wisconsin Supreme Court Justice Louis Butler. Butler, a former public defender who had been appointed to fill a vacancy in 2004 by Democratic governor Jim Doyle, was the first Black justice on Wisconsin's highest court. In 2008 Butler was seeking election to a full ten-year term on the court.

Gableman ran as an avowed conservative. Although Wisconsin law does not allow judges to proclaim a party affiliation, Republicans campaigned for Gableman while Democrats supported Butler. Both sides knew the stakes were high. If Gableman were elected, he would tip the court's balance from liberal to conservative.

Gableman won a narrow victory, garnering 51 percent of the vote after one of the most contentious and most expensive judicial races in the state's history up to that point. For the first time in over forty years, a challenger defeated a sitting justice in Wisconsin. (The last incumbent to lose a reelection bid had been blamed for letting a popular sports team leave the state.) Gableman assumed his seat on the Wisconsin Supreme Court on August 1, 2008. That was only the beginning of the story.

In March 2008, just weeks before the election, Gableman's campaign had run a television advertisement attacking Butler. With eerie music playing, the ad showed pictures of two Black men: Justice Butler side by side with a mug shot of his former client, Reuben Lee Mitchell, who had twice been convicted of sexually assaulting children. The transcript of the narrator's commentary read in full:

> Unbelievable. Shadowy special interests supporting Louis Butler are attacking Judge Michael Gableman. It's not true!
>
> Judge, District Attorney, Michael Gableman has committed his life to locking up criminals to keep families safe—putting child molesters behind bars for over 100 years.
>
> Louis Butler worked to put criminals on the street.
>
> Like Reuben Lee Mitchell, who raped an 11-year-old girl with learning disabilities. Butler found a loophole. Mitchell went on to molest another child.
>
> Can Wisconsin families feel safe with Louis Butler on the Supreme Court?[32]

What had Louis Butler actually done?

Butler had worked as a public defender from 1979 to 1992. In that capacity he was appointed to represent Mitchell. On appeal of Mitchell's conviction for raping a child, Butler successfully argued that the state had violated an evidentiary rule by allowing the prosecution to introduce the fact that the rape victim had been a virgin. However, the Wisconsin Supreme Court subsequently declared the evidentiary error harmless, and Mitchell remained in prison until he was released on parole in the normal course of events. The oral narration to Gableman's advertisement was accompanied by writing, including citations to opinions in Mitchell's case, which point-edly omitted the Supreme Court opinion that kept Mitchell in prison.

To many contemporaneous observers, including more than fifty Wisconsin judges, the ad seemed obviously false and misleading as well as racially charged. Thirty-five sitting Wisconsin judges signed a statement charging that the ad fell outside "the bounds of fairness, honesty and integrity for candidates running for judicial office." Another seventeen sitting judges signed similar public letters.[33]

Comparisons to the Willie Horton ad that helped put President George H. W. Bush in office are hard to avoid. Both ads include racial dog whistles, a law and order drumbeat, and misleading attributions of responsibility for crimes committed by others. Gableman wrongfully accused his opponent of using a legal "loophole" to get the rapist of an eleven-year-old girl out of prison and charged that Butler's successful representation led inexorably to his client's sexual assault on another child. In fact, Butler's client served his entire term in prison, including years when Butler was already on the state's highest court.

Shortly after the election, a group that had supported Butler's campaign asked the state's Judicial Commission, which is charged with investigating allegations of judicial misconduct, to look into the ad. Gableman was subject to the state's judicial code of ethics as a sitting judge and as a candidate for judicial office.

Following an investigation, on October 7, 2008, the Judicial Commission filed a formal complaint against Gableman with the Supreme Court on which Gableman now sat. The complaint alleged that Gableman had willfully violated the Code of Judicial Conduct's rules governing judicial contests.

The Code adopted the latest American Bar Association standards. It applied only to what the candidates themselves said or authorized others to say on their behalf. Two rules addressed factual misrepresentations. The Code distinguished between false statements of fact, which were strictly forbidden ("shall not"), and true statements that knowingly mislead, a purely aspirational ("should not") recommendation. The distinction would turn out to be critical.

Gableman, Act Two, Scene One

Following normal procedures, the Wisconsin Supreme Court referred the matter to the chief judge of the Court of Appeals, who convened a three-judge Judicial Conduct Panel to consider the allegations. The panel recommended that the Supreme Court dismiss the ethics complaint.

As an initial matter, the panel emphasized that Justice Butler did not bear any responsibility for his client's release from prison or his subsequent crimes: "Nothing that Justice Butler did in the course of his representation of Mitchell caused, facilitated, or enabled Mitchell's release from prison in 1992." Nor did any aspect of Butler's representation of Mitchell have "any connection to Mitchell's commission of a second sexual assault of a child."[34]

Given the panel's factual conclusions, why did it dismiss the ethical complaint stemming from Gableman's ad?

The three judges, who could not agree on how to analyze the legal questions, issued three separate opinions. Two of the judges took a formalistic approach. They concluded that each of the statements in the ad was factually correct, even if in the aggregate they proved misleading. They blamed the Code's language for letting Gableman off the hook. The Code seemed to require a penalty for false factual representations, while merely advising judges not to promulgate factually true but misleading statements, the kind of lie I call an intentional distortion.

One of those two judges also wrote separately to underscore that "no one should be misled into believing that we find no fault with the advertisement." Gableman's counsel had "virtually conceded" at oral argument, he pointed out, that the ad "falsely implies that Justice Butler's representation of Reuben Mitchell caused or resulted in Mitchell's release from prison," violating what he regarded as the "'aspirational'" part of the Code. Gableman's attorney had admitted that the aspirational portion of the Code applied because the ad was a "classic example" of a communication in which "three or four truthful statements . . . are misleading because of a key fact that is omitted."

That concurrence also condemned the ad for confusing the public about the proper role of attorneys in an adversary system. Lawyers are required to provide exactly the sort of zealous representation that Butler gave his client, including searching for any loopholes statutes or judicial opinions have left open. The judge concluded ironically, "Justice Gableman has been represented in this matter by an able lawyer who, it might be argued, 'found a loophole.'"

The third judge—Ralph Adam Fine—agreed that the complaint against Gableman should be dismissed but took issue with every other point. Judge Fine believed the Code violated the First Amendment, and that it unconstitutionally seized for the government the power to condemn campaign speech, a power that in his view the Constitution reserved for the voters.

Judge Fine emphasized that if he had accepted the proposition that the state could penalize campaign speech without violating the Constitution, he would have found that Gableman knowingly misrepresented the facts. The ad pointed to only one conclusion—that Butler's representation "permitted Mitchell to commit the later sex crime." That inference was intended, and clearly false. Like others before and since, Judge Fine pointed to George Orwell's Ministry of Truth: "The notion that the government, rather than the people, may be the final arbiter of truth in political debate is fundamentally at odds with the First Amendment."

The two other panelists limited their consideration of First Amendment issues to a footnote, but they agreed Gableman's right to free expression would have been implicated if they had found that the Code applied to his misrepresentations. To avoid any constitutional issues, they "narrowly" interpreted the Code to reach "only" bald-faced lies, "representations of fact that are clearly and blatantly false."[35] If that interpretation is correct, Wisconsin's Judicial Code of Conduct would be severely deficient because it leaves so much falsehood unregulated.

Gableman, Act Two, Scene Two

When the matter reached the Wisconsin Supreme Court for review in 2010, the six justices who participated in the decision after Gableman recused himself unanimously rejected his argument that the state's framework regulating falsehoods during judicial campaigns violated the First Amendment.[36]

The unanimity was deceptive because the court was bitterly—and evenly—divided over whether Gableman's advertisement constituted a misrepresentation of fact. Like comparative literature scholars, they disputed how to interpret a text: Should each component of the text be treated as a separate publication, or should they assess the impact the video had on viewers when taken as a whole? More broadly, they could not reach consensus on how to define objective truth or, perhaps, on whether such a concept exists.

Chief Justice Shirley Abrahamson, writing for the three justices in the court's liberal wing, took the position that one could not, as the specially appointed judicial panel below and the three remaining justices did, "read each of the sentences . . . in isolation, as if the other sentences did not exist." A myopic focus on literal truth, she asserted, denudes each sentence of "context or meaning." The message as a whole communicated that "Butler's actions in representing Mitchell and finding a 'loophole' led to Mitchell's release and his commission of another crime. No other reasonable interpretation of the advertisement has been suggested. . . . This message is objectively false."[37] Like Judge Fine concurring below, they would have held Gableman responsible for what I have called intentional distortion. Abrahamson's opinion (signed by the two other liberal justices) recommended pursuing the matter through a jury trial in a lower court to determine what the advertisement meant.

Justice David Prosser's separate opinion, co-signed by the two other conservative judges who participated, took the position that each sentence was immune from penalty because each statement in isolation was "objectively true." The Prosser opinion treated the disputed text as if it were a series of tweets spun out over days or weeks that had no contextual connection to each other. Each sentence, Prosser concluded, contained verifiable facts.[38]

The two opinions for an evenly divided court—a three-to-three tie—were handled in a way that I have never seen before in over thirty-five years of reading opinions. The opinions were published separately, one after the other, as distinct opinions with separate citations in the official case records.

Because neither opinion mustered a majority, the upshot was that the decision of the panel below remained in place: the ethics complaint against Gableman was dismissed.

Gableman, Act Three

Gableman remained on the Wisconsin Supreme Court. President Obama nominated Butler for a federal judgeship, but the nomination died in the Senate. It fell victim to Republican then–Senate Majority Leader Mitch McConnell's determination to bring as few as possible of President Obama's judicial nominees to the floor for a vote. Butler entered private practice in Wisconsin.

By 2011, the hyper-partisanship that had prevented shared understanding of the Gableman case had escalated so much that two of the women justices on the court feared for their safety. According to news accounts,

Chief Justice Shirley Abrahamson and Justice Ann Walsh Bradley reported that Justice Prosser was growing increasingly menacing. They worried about whether they were safe at work. Law enforcement officials, noting an escalating pattern of disturbing behavior, provided their emergency contact numbers to the two justices and advised them not to be in their offices outside normal work hours without locking their doors and alerting the police.

Matters came to a head on July 13, 2011, the night before the court announced another bitterly divided opinion—this time involving controversial legislation sponsored by the state's Republicans that rolled back collective bargaining rights for public employees, a matter that had attracted national attention while Scott Walker was governor. Six of the seven justices had gathered in Justice Bradley's office for a last conversation about the 4–3 vote on party lines, when Bradley asked Prosser to leave.

All of the participants agree a bitter argument ensued. By one account, Prosser tried to choke Bradley. By another, she entered his space, and in trying to ward her off, Prosser's hand landed around her neck. Although Prosser admitted his hands "landed" on Bradley's neck, he disputed how that happened. Justice Gableman defended Prosser—who had saved *his* neck in the disciplinary proceeding—by telling investigators that Prosser's hands were "never" around Bradley's neck. A criminal investigation followed, but no charges resulted.[39]

The Judicial Commission recommended disciplinary action against Prosser, but because the three remaining conservative justices recused themselves it proved impossible to muster the quorum needed for the court to act. Prosser remained on the court until 2016.

In June 2017 Gableman announced that he would not seek reelection in 2018.

The Gableman story contains a number of cautionary tales about why it is so difficult to enforce regulations that prohibit campaign lies, even in the rare instance that the laws survive a First Amendment challenge.

First, even though the facts were straightforward, the judges disagreed about what the facts meant. Justice Abrahamson's opinion found it beyond argument that the video was "objectively false," which would make it a bald-faced lie.

The advertisement was not an impromptu misstatement. Gableman personally approved the ad before it ran. Later, he admitted that when he first saw the ad, he was unsure whether he should allow it to run. He spent a week mulling over the decision. In most instances, everyone agreed, such underhanded maneuvers are left to allies, like PACs, outside the candidate's direct control, in order to ensure deniability.

Although Gableman had "virtually conceded" through counsel at the Judicial Conduct Panel that the advertisement was "misleading,"[40] it proved impossible to achieve consensus on where the line should be drawn between technical truth and genuine falsehood.

Recall that courts have drawn fine lines in defamation cases involving public figures when discussing how "far removed from the truth" a statement must be in order to "permit an inference of actual malice, even assuming arguendo [a statement] was false." A speaker will be held liable in defamation where "the substance, the gist, the sting" of the communication taken as a whole, is patently false.[41]

The three justices who signed Chief Justice Abrahamson's opinion found the full statement in context bore no resemblance to truth.

Justice Prossser and his two cosigners, in contrast, appeared to give more weight to the proposition in defamation law that if a statement "is 'substantially' true in overall effect, minor inaccuracies or falsities will not create falsity." Under the substantial truth doctrine, if the gist of the defamatory statement "is not so very different from the 'truth,'" then "campaign rhetoric" is protected.[42]

It is hard to see how the independent facts strung together in Gableman's advertisement looked anything like the truth. No one even suggested the ad was "'substantially' true in overall effect." The overall impact of Gableman's ad, as Gableman's attorney had conceded, was patently false. Prosser and his cosigners appear to have been substantially confused, to put it charitably.

Second, the liar may be an incumbent, with connections to decision makers. Imagine how uncomfortable the six justices on the Wisconsin Supreme Court must have been sitting in judgment on a colleague they saw every workday.

Third, partisanship appears to have encouraged the signers of Prosser's opinion to put preservation of Gableman's seat on the court above concern about the court's credibility and integrity. If that was not clear at the time, Prosser's subsequent choking of a liberal justice indicates just how far the bench had strayed from its theoretically nonpartisan posture. A court that had once been held out as a model state appellate court found its reputation in tatters.

Fourth, a regulatory structure designed to sustain the integrity of the judicial system allowed a misleading advertisement for a person seeking the highest judicial office to materially undermine public understanding of the adversary system. Gableman had urged voters to hold an appointed lawyer personally responsible for the later actions of a client the lawyer was required to represent zealously.

Chief Justice Abrahamson feared that the court's refusal to remand the matter for a jury trial to ascertain whether the advertisement violated the judicial code invited "future judicial candidates to push and distort the content of advertising in judicial campaigns as far past truthful communication as the creative use of language may allow."[43] If the advertisement, taken as a whole, did not amount to a bald-faced lie, it surely was an intentional distortion, or, at a minimum, an indirect prevarication resting on contextual distortion that was intended to deceive voters.

The *Gableman* saga indicates that even if the First Amendment posed no obstacle to regulating campaign falsehood, and even if a regulatory scheme survived strict scrutiny, it could still prove virtually impossible for regulators to agree about where the boundaries between truth and falsehood should be drawn. If regulation of campaign lies were constitutionally permissible, which I have argued it is not, such rules would hold little promise of offering a panacea. Since *Gableman* indicates that bald-faced defamatory statements about opponents disguised as factoids are not amenable to regulation, the normative message to partisans seems to be: use innuendo with abandon.

While the First Amendment and definitional challenges make legal regulation untenable, there is powerful social value in combating falsehood. The task of exposing campaign lies is properly shared by the target of the lies and the press. The ultimate arbiters must be the voters. But it is only possible to punish liars at the ballot box if citizens are engaged enough to sort through disinformation, and if voters conclude that lying matters.

CHAPTER 5

Viral Lies:
Life and Death in the COVID-19 Era

We have seen the formidable constitutional and definitional barriers to regulating verifiable factual falsehoods. We have reviewed the constitutional doctrine and the philosophical underpinnings that gave rise to those barriers, among them apprehension about the societal risks of a government empowered to punish falsehood. But such concerns do not assuage the dangers that unchecked falsehoods present to society.

This chapter considers whether the harm that ensued from President Trump's lies about the 2020 pandemic would overcome the First Amendment obstacles to punishing falsehoods. From *United States* v. *Alvarez*, we know that "something more" than a lie is required. I argue in this chapter that the president's falsehoods, and the death and illness that flowed from them, surpass any understanding of the harm needed to show "something more." With just 4 percent of the world's population, each month from June through December 2020 the United States sustained an average of roughly 20 percent of all the world's infections.[1] Presidential lies contributed enormously to delayed and deficient federal responses and, above all, to popular complacency and social division that made a cohesive response all but impossible.

Three threads overlap in my analysis of Trump's lethal coronavirus deceptions: first, Trump's outright lies and denials of verifiable facts combined with remarkable explosive truths, admissions which prove that he knew he was lying; second, his administration's suppression and delegitimation of science; and third, the wake of devastation attributable in large part to

Trump's falsehoods. I leave it to others to analyze Trump's administrative and policy failings in response to the pandemic.

Trump Knew

What did President Trump know, and when did he know it? The answer is crucial to determining whether Trump knowingly lied to the American public about the risks posed by COVID-19, about the need to protect ourselves, and about potential remedies. Thanks to journalist Bob Woodward, a hero of the Watergate era, that is no longer a mystery we need to investigate.

In September 2020, Woodward revealed that on January 28 in the Oval Office, national security adviser Robert O'Brien alerted the president, "This is going to be the biggest national security threat to your presidency."[2] Trump later claimed he had no memory of that warning.

Other administration officials had also warned the president about the grave dangers posed by the coronavirus. Peter Navarro, Trump's trade adviser, circulated a memo to the president and other high-level officials, urgently calling for an aggressive response to the coronavirus. Lacking a cure or vaccine, Navarro insisted in January, Americans would be "defenseless in the case of a full-blown coronavirus outbreak . . . imperiling the lives of millions of Americans." In a second memo a month later Navarro sounded even graver alarms: there is, he wrote, an "increasing probability of a full-blown COVID-19 pandemic that could infect as many as 100 million Americans, with a loss of life of as many as 1–2 million souls."[3]

In subsequent public statements Trump proclaimed ignorance, declaring, "Nobody knew that a thing like this could happen."[4]

Who could have known? Anybody who was paying attention. Reports of the novel virus reached Dr. Anthony Fauci, the nation's leading expert on infectious diseases, and Dr. Robert Redfield, head of the Centers for Disease Control (CDC), in late December 2019 just days after SARS-CoV-2 was first identified in Wuhan, China. Both geared up.

On January 21, 2020, the first case in the United States was announced in the state of Washington. Three days later, the prestigious medical journal the *Lancet* reported preliminary evidence of person-to-person transmission.

By January 27, 2020, with just five cases identified in the United States, former vice president Joe Biden published an op-ed in *USA Today* entitled "Trump Is Worst Possible Leader to Deal with Coronavirus Outbreak."

Biden warned that it will "get worse before it gets better" and underscored that the United States was unprepared for a "dangerous epidemic that will come sooner or later."[5]

As Woodward's audiotapes of Trump's explosive truthful admissions, released on September 9, 2020, confirmed, Trump had early, sobering knowledge of COVID's threats. On February 7, 2020, about one month after China announced a new coronavirus spreading in Wuhan, when there were only twelve confirmed cases in the United States, Trump confided in Woodward: the virus "is a very tricky situation. . . . You just breathe air and that's how it's passed. . . . It's also more deadly than even your strenuous flus." Trump emphasized the virus's potential to blow everything up: "There's dynamite behind every door."[6]

And yet that same month, Trump was telling audiences the virus "miraculously goes away" when it gets "a little warmer." He claimed the disease was "very much under control" in the United States, a claim he would repeat going forward. By late summer, when warming weather had not made the virus disappear, Trump's mantra became "We're rounding the corner."

On March 19, after COVID-19 had reached 114 countries and the World Health Organization (WHO) had officially declared it a "pandemic," Trump tried to justify to Woodward his false reassurances to the public. He admitted that he did not want to level with the American people. He thought the public would panic rather than rising to the emergency. Trump also relayed to Woodward the "startling facts" scientists had conveyed to him: COVID-19 strikes young people too, a fact he would repeatedly refute in later public statements.[7]

At his daily coronavirus briefing two days after that conversation, Trump again misled the public about how dangerous the pandemic was: "Stay calm. It will go away."[8] He knew better.

Trump never leveled with the American public. He continued to downplay the severity of the virus. As time passed, he began to deny that the virus existed, even after he was hospitalized with it, calling the pandemic a politically motivated "hoax."

Your Lying Eyes: Bare Faces

Trump's intentionally dishonest denials discouraged many individuals from taking precautions for themselves and for the benefit of their neighbors. His refusal to wear a face mask reinforced his mendacious claim. The bare face became a political performance.

Trump played a disproportionate role in introducing falsehoods into the COVID conversation. Researchers at Cornell University who analyzed thirty-eight million English-language print and online articles about the pandemic found that Trump was responsible for an astounding nearly 38 percent of *all* the misinformation about COVID-19. Sarah Evanega, the lead author, called Trump "the single largest driver of misinformation around COVID." Most of the misinformation Trump spread concerned the "'miracle'" cures he promoted, adding to the urgency of Evanega's concern about the "real-world dire health implications" of his factual falsehoods.[9]

Trump's most devoted followers believed him at their peril, as Kristin Urquiza, whose sixty-five-year-old father died of COVID-19 during the summer of 2020, eloquently explained. Speaking at the Democratic National Convention, Urquiza charged that her father had "believed" the president's assurances that the virus "was under control and going to disappear, that it was OK to end social distancing rules before it was safe, and that if you had no underlying health conditions you'd probably be fine." When Arizona ended its stay-at-home order in late May, Mark Anthony Urquiza joined some friends at a karaoke bar. He was soon on a ventilator, and, like many others, he died in an ICU without his family. His daughter's punch line hit home: Mark Anthony's "only pre-existing condition was trusting Donald Trump—and for that he paid with his life."[10]

Trump endangered his supporters in other ways too. For example, he gathered large mask-less crowds at cramped campaign rallies up until Election Day. Oblivious to evidence of a rise in cases after his rallies, Trump denied anyone had been infected at those events: "We've had no negative effect and we've had 35 to 40,000 people" at the rallies.[11]

Both parts of that statement were untrue. The crowds hovered at several thousand attendees, not tens of thousands. And substantiated cases had been traced to Trump's first large rally of the campaign season, held in Tulsa, Oklahoma. The president seemed to have forgotten that his "friend," former presidential primary candidate Herman Cain, had died of COVID-19 shortly after attending the Tulsa rally. A study of data from the ten weeks following eighteen Trump rallies by a group at Stanford University confirmed the suspicion that the rallies were "superspreader" events that had led to more than thirty thousand additional confirmed cases of COVID-19 and "likely led to more than 700 deaths."[12]

Trump's acolytes endangered themselves at large gatherings beyond campaign events. In August 2020, for example, roughly 460,000 bikers from every state in the nation headed to Sturgis, South Dakota for an annual rally where they gathered unconstrained by masks or social distancing. Many wore shirts that proclaimed attendance as an act of defiance directed at state-imposed masking regulations. The *New York Times* estimated that "at least 300" casualties resulted from the rally, including those who attended, those back home who caught it from them, and residents of Sturgis.[13] South Dakota soon became one of the hottest of COVID-19 hot zones in the United States.

The High Cost of Signaling and Other Political Performance

Why would so many people risk their lives by foregoing simple preventive measures like wearing a mask and practicing social distancing? One answer might be that Trump asked them to. Harvard psychologist Joshua Greene posits that "costly signals" of loyalty to a coalition require that members make themselves "irredeemably unacceptable to the other tribe." The most useful differential signals, Greene explains, are those that others would never adopt. This renders "practical and functional truths . . . generally useless" as a group statement.[14] That is one reason Trump's continued misdirection unified his diehard supporters with the bonus that it expressed scorn for everyone else and exposed the entire population to contamination.

That was not enough for Trump, who pressed further: coronavirus, he asserted, "affects virtually nobody. It's an amazing thing." Trump uttered those words at a rally in Ohio in late September as the United States, which had the dubious honor of leading the world in the number of deaths and cases for months, passed the milestone of two hundred thousand deaths. And he once again falsely claimed that the disease only hurt "elderly people with heart problems and other problems. . . . Below the age of 18, like nobody."[15]

Trump baselessly asserted COVID-19 would disappear right after the election when, he charged, Democrats would no longer need it to make him look bad. But he kept contradicting himself right up until the election. On the one hand, he asserted the virus was a hoax, and on the other, he insisted the nonexistent virus was "under control." Meanwhile, the daily numbers of new cases kept breaking previous records. We are "rounding" the curve, Trump and his delegates repeated, as if saying it could make it true. All the while, the seven-day moving average daily death toll and the number of new cases continued to soar.

On Our Own

Initially, those who were not true believers were left to their own devices as they searched for guidance. In the geographical areas of the United States hit early and hard by COVID-19, many people took precautions long before the government urged measures like staying home. Individuals could control preventive measures like hand-washing, staying home, and later, when new recommendations emerged, wearing masks. They could not control what was happening (and not happening) around them.

Trump took at best a cavalier approach to providing accurate information to the public, similar to the approach he would later display when he retweeted a QAnon conspiracy theory that claimed President Obama had staged a fake execution of Osama bin Laden and murdered the Navy SEAL Team 6 members to cover up the deception. Confronted by NBC's Savannah Guthrie about why he would share a transparent lie, Trump responded "That was a retweet. . . . I'll put it out there. People can decide for themselves."[16]

That same approach—let the people sort it out—characterized many of Trump's dangerous claims about COVID-19. Even as he announced new CDC guidance about masking on April 3, 2020, Trump denigrated and undermined it: "But this is voluntary. I don't think I'm going to be doing it. . . . So with the masks, it's going to be, really, a voluntary thing. You can do it. You don't have to do it. I'm choosing not to do it. . . . It's only a recommendation."[17]

Basic psychological dynamics amplified people's vulnerability to Trump's lies. As scholars of decision making have explained, the human brain prefers clarity. When a situation is unprecedented, people whose circles have been spared direct experience of risk are likely to misgauge its magnitude when they lack clear instructions from trustworthy leaders. That need for trustworthy information was especially urgent in the early days of the pandemic. Difficulty in perceiving risk accurately is compounded by what psychologists call "optimism bias"—a protective instinct to expect a rosier outcome than the available information might suggest. Trump's dishonesty deprived Americans of the game plan each individual desperately needed.[18]

Snake Oil and Demon Sperm

Trump promoted the use of dangerous products, including bleach and hydroxychloroquine, as home remedies. Some gullible people actually tried bleach, while others clogged COVID-19 hotlines seeking details. A few days after Trump first declared the medication a "gamechanger," an Arizona couple who had listened to him ingested a fish tank cleanser containing chloroquine in an effort to ward off the virus; the man died. Facing criticism, Trump recanted, claiming he was just joking, being sarcastic, about bleach. The video belied that specious defense.

Trump repeatedly urged people to ask their doctors for the antimalarial drug hydroxychloroquine, the equivalent of snake oil when used for COVID-19. Trump pressed people to use hydroxychloroquine long after the findings from an early study promoting its use had been quickly retracted by the journal that had published it.

No matter—under Trump's advocacy demand for the drug soared. The CDC found an *eightyfold* increase in prescriptions for the medication in the early months of 2020 compared to the year before. That inflated demand led to serious shortages of the drug, temporarily depriving patients worldwide of their usual medication.[19]

Hyping hydroxychloroquine at the daily coronavirus briefings he held in the spring, Trump assured the public "it's not going to kill anybody," and added rhetorically, "What do you have to lose?" The answer was not long in coming. By the end of April, the Food and Drug Administration (FDA) warned that hydroxychloroquine could cause arrhythmia and sudden cardiac death. Concerned about adverse effects, NIH and the WHO each canceled controlled studies of the drug, while the FDA, the CDC, and major medical associations all issued warnings about its risks.[20]

In July, Trump retweeted a news conference full of specious claims by Dr. Stella Immanuel that far-right Breitbart News had livestreamed. Immanuel's quackery included claims that hydroxychloroquine would "cure" COVID-19; that masks were not needed; and, most famously, that "demon sperm" from "spirit" spouses causes human ailments. As social media and cable channels amplified this craziness, Trump sidestepped: "I thought her voice was an important voice, but I know nothing about her."[21]

Denying Viral Spread

Trump continued to lie about COVID-19 after he was diagnosed with it and entered Walter Reed Hospital, where he came close to being placed on a ventilator. Although he had told Woodward this virus "is a killer if it gets you," after being released from the hospital he exhorted Americans, "Don't let it dominate you" shortly after he dramatically ripped off his mask as he returned to the White House.[22]

Trump denied throughout that COVID-19 threatened children. He insisted that children were immune to the virus, even as nearly one hundred thousand children tested positive during just the last two weeks of July when Trump was urging schools to open for the fall term. Facebook removed Trump's false claim that children are "virtually immune" because it contained "harmful COVID misinformation."[23]

Trump then reframed his statements to say that in the rare case in which children caught the virus, they did not spread it to others, "certainly not very easily," and they got "better very quickly." He conceded that there may be "a tiny fraction of death." Pressed by a reporter, Trump said, "Yeah," he believed that "children are essentially immune."[24]

Contradicting Trump's assertions about children, the American Academy of Pediatrics reported that by October 22, children accounted for 11 percent of all confirmed COVID-19 cases in the United States (almost eight hundred thousand children had tested positive for the virus). It underscored that the disease could be fatal for children, even though they were less likely than adults to be hospitalized or die.[25]

By Election Day, where this account ends, every area of the country was afflicted. During the preceding weeks, cases reached new heights in half of all US counties. Hospitals in both rural and urban locations were at or nearing capacity. Testing capacity and supplies for personal protective equipment were running short, as they had in the spring when the major outbreaks were confined to a more limited geographical area.[26]

Despite medical progress in treating the disease, at least when hospitals were not over capacity, death rates were also rising. During October about a third of the counties in the United States reported record deaths from COVID-19. Scientists predicted deaths would mount, growing just behind hospitalizations. Later events proved them right. By early December the number of new cases each day topped two hundred thousand. That number crested at over three hundred thousand on January 8, 2021, the week before Trump left office.

Science Denial

Suppression of data gathering, data sharing, and scientifically reliable information presents another form of the verifiable falsehoods that characterized Trump's pandemic response. It impeded scientific progress and encouraged disbelief of expert messages, dooming a rational response to the pandemic.

Dr. Fauci versus the Pretenders

Disparagement of expert knowledge has a long pedigree in the United States. Alexis de Tocqueville had linked democratic ideals to Americans' confidence in their own reasoning as the "source of truth," since all persons are equal. The historian Richard Hofstadter, writing in 1963, explained that the increasing complexity of modern life had stripped Americans of that naïve confidence: now they knew they could not attain the competence to understand all that surrounded them. They resented the inadequacy they recognized, as well as the elite experts on whom they were increasingly forced to rely.

More recently, as Tom Nichols argued in *The Death of Expertise*, the United States and other industrialized nations have witnessed "a positive *hostility*" to "established knowledge," leading to the insistence that one person's opinions are as good as another's verifiable facts. In 2016 Trump not only benefited from that hostility; he was, according to Nichols, a "one-man campaign against established knowledge."[27]

If Trump genuinely did not understand or believe in science, it could be argued that the stream of deception and obfuscation that flowed from repressing data would not qualify as "lies" because he would have lacked the requisite intent to deceive. But Trump's private conversations prove he knew he was lying in public—he left the sort of evidence that lawyers call an "admission against interest" at a trial.

Trump's attacks on expertise continued unabated after he became president and reached a crescendo when COVID-19 struck. In the early days of the pandemic, and again as he grew more impatient with the prolonged crisis, Trump relied heavily on people who may have been experts at *something* but had no special knowledge about viral diseases.

Early on, Trump's inner circle took guidance from an article published on March 16, 2020, by University of Chicago law professor Richard Epstein on the website of the conservative Hoover Institution at Stanford University. Epstein, a libertarian who takes a law and economics approach to most problems, argued that people were vastly overreacting to a perceived threat. His perspective fed into Trump's instinct that he needed to keep the economy running full steam to win reelection. Epstein predicted that about five hundred people might die in the United States. (He later raised the estimate to five thousand while Dr. Fauci was dramatically underestimating the fatalities at one hundred thousand to two hundred thousand total deaths).

Epstein is a legal scholar, but expertise is not transferrable no matter how much the arrogant might wish it were so. He asserted that his "skill of cross-examination" prepared him to question epidemiological findings. Medical professionals contradicted many of Epstein's declarations (for example, there are "milder" forms of COVID-19, or that syphilis—caused by bacteria—provides a useful analogy for a viral illness). Epstein then reframed his work as "a theory," adding, "If that's wrong, somebody should tell me." They had.[28]

Trump and his team seized on Epstein's writing to downplay the virus and to justify giving priority to maintaining a churning economy. They failed to recognize that controlling the pandemic was a prerequisite for meaningful economic recovery.

By August 2020, Trump had sidelined the leading experts on his coronavirus task force, including Drs. Deborah Birx and Anthony Fauci, and brought in Dr. Scott Atlas, a neuroradiologist at Stanford's Hoover Institution. Atlas had no experience with infectious diseases. He had, however, appeared on Fox News shows where he had pushed an agenda that appealed to Trump's instincts: less testing, insistence that studies promoting masks were "garbage," and that the economy should not be shut down.

Atlas's monopolization of the president's ear prompted alarm. Fauci worried aloud that Atlas was feeding Trump "incorrect" information. CDC

Director Robert Redfield was overheard charging that "everything" Atlas says is "false." One anonymous senior administration official confirmed that Trump "wants to use yes-men to discredit the reputations of truth tellers."[29]

Suppressing Data

While visiting the CDC on March 7, Trump, in a rare moment of transparency, indulged in another explosive truth. He explained why he would not allow infected passengers to disembark the *Grand Princess* cruise ship. "I like the numbers being where they are. I don't need to have the numbers double because of one ship."[30]

Trump attributed a rise in reported infections to expanded testing, which he misleadingly called the best testing in the world. In fact, the scale of testing did not explain why at the end of October the United States had three times more coronavirus cases than the European Union, which has a population roughly one-third larger than ours.

Trump persisted in charging that testing inflated the number of infections. "Instead of 25 million tests," Trump posited, "let's say we did 10 million tests. We'd look like we were doing much better because we'd have far fewer cases," he told CBN News.[31]

The night before the election, Trump tweeted yet again: "We have more Cases because we have more Testing!" *Washington Post* fact-checker Glenn Kessler responded, "Not only is this dumb, but the USA still does not rank in the top ten countries in terms of testing per million people."[32]

Trump's obtuseness about testing and his efforts to discourage it aligned with his administration's efforts to dismantle long-established systems for gathering data, impeding public health efforts. The administration abruptly relieved the CDC of the responsibility for collecting information from hospitals, substituting a small private firm supervised by the Department of Health and Human Services (HHS). *Science*, a highly respected journal, later reported that the HHS figures "often diverge dramatically from those collected by the other federal source, from state-supplied data, and from the apparent reality on the ground."[33]

Representative Jim Clyburn, chair of the House Select Subcommittee on the Coronavirus Crisis, slammed "President Trump's contempt for science" as he charged the administration with hiding the information it still collected. Clyburn released six of the White House Coronavirus Task Force's weekly reports that had been concealed from the public which revealed spiking positivity rates following the Labor Day weekend.[34]

Christopher J. L. Murray, director of the Institute for Health Metrics and Evaluation at the University of Washington, which produces many of the studies and projections the government and epidemiologists rely on, issued an impassioned plea that the government release detailed data in its possession. The data were needed to facilitate epidemiological research that could help determine how best to manage the spiraling pandemic.[35]

The lies, the twisting of data, and the refusal to release reliable information all undermined faith in science (already at a low among the portion of Americans who reject global warming and reliable vaccinations for childhood diseases).

Trump eviscerated any basis for the trust that psychologists say people must have for government leaders if the state is to protect the population. In mid-March 2020, when the pandemic had just started, only 37 percent of people asked by an NPR/PBS NewsHour/Marist poll how much they trusted the information they heard about coronavirus from President Trump replied that they trusted it "a great deal" or "a good amount." Since Trump's floor of support never fell below the mid-thirties, it seems only his hard-core partisans believed him even at the outset. By a week before the election, an Axios/Ipsos poll found that only 29 percent trusted Trump "a great deal" or "a fair amount" to provide "accurate information about coronavirus."[36]

A *New York Times*/Siena College survey administered in mid-October 2020 found that nearly two-thirds of respondents opposed a national mandate to take an FDA-approved coronavirus vaccine. The profound lack of trust in Trump's veracity seemed to augur badly for the chances that a vaccine approved and marketed before the end of Trump's administration would be widely accepted.[37]

The Wake of Destruction

Presidential lies that demolished trust, amplified by the failures of the administrative state and denigration of science, caused almost incomprehensible concrete harms. I will discuss only some of the most dramatic: deaths, chronic illness, and economic devastation.

Death and Chronic Illness

As Election Day 2020 neared, when more than 230,000 people in the United States had died of COVID-19, Trump accused the "fake news" of exaggerating the significance of the COVID-19 statistics in order to attack him. He falsely charged that when passenger planes carrying five hundred people crashed no one paid any attention.[38] But the number of deaths attributed to the virus between February and the end of October 2020 would have equaled five hundred large plane crashes, or roughly two planes a day falling from the sky with no survivors. That would attract anyone's attention.

Other constructs also help us to grasp the enormity of the losses. Commentators noted that the total US COVID-19 deaths in late September (under two hundred thousand at that point) equaled all of the American lives lost in three major wars combined: World War I, the Korean War, and the Vietnam War. A Harvard Medical School report calculated the loss this way: the 194,000 US deaths from COVID-19 when the study was performed meant that over "2,500,000 person-years of life" had been lost. On average, the deceased lost over thirteen years of life, with variances by gender and age.[39]

Trump's knowingly false public denials proved deadly. A statistical simulation from Columbia University published in *Science* concluded that if the United States had implemented social distancing and isolation just one week earlier than it did, at least thirty-two thousand lives would have been saved, roughly half of them in New York City alone. Acting two weeks earlier would have saved almost sixty thousand lives and reduced the case count by over one million. Scientific models projected that tens of thousands of lives could have been saved if at least 95 percent of Americans had worn masks in public.[40]

The brute fact of death also fails to capture the scope of loss. A British public health professor months into her illness emphasized its impact on the "quality of life." Death, she urged, "is not the only thing that counts. We must also count lives changed." Months into the pandemic, studies confirmed anecdotal evidence that a substantial proportion of COVID-19 survivors were "long-haulers," with tens of thousands of Americans suffering from "lingering illness" three months into a bout of COVID-19.[41]

The symptoms long-haulers display include profound exhaustion, cough-ing, and brain fog as well as "permanent damage to their lungs, heart, kidneys, or brain" that affects their ability to function. Some will be unable to hold jobs or carry out the daily tasks of life. They may not be able to qualify for disability payments because their disease is not well understood or easily proven.[42]

But the loss transcends the tangible and physical. The raw numbers fail to capture the human loss "in the form of emotional and economic tolls . . . on the families, friends and co-workers of those lost. Who among us would not cherish another 5 years together with a father, mother, son, daughter or close friend?"[43] Those lost hours kept mounting as death numbers rose.

As often happens after large-scale traumatic events, COVID-19 exacer-bated the incidence of mental illness. For instance, one study showed rates of depression three times higher than before COVID-19 struck. Oxford research-ers who reviewed medical records for almost seventy million patients in the United States found even more startling effects: between fourteen and ninety days after being diagnosed with COVID-19, more than one in five COVID-19 survivors reported psychiatric disorders, dementia, and/or insomnia.[44]

Economic Devastation

Other research confirmed what common sense suggests: the mental anguish during the pandemic was highly correlated to the economic hardship that spread through all regions of the country as a direct result of COVID-19. Most public health experts and economists agreed that the economic fallout from the pandemic could not be remedied until the virus itself was brought under control. The devastation included dramatic levels of un- and under-employment, growing food and housing insecurity, and rising poverty rates.

Twenty-two million jobs disappeared almost overnight when the pan-demic began to spread on both coasts in March and into April 2020. That equals the number of jobs lost during the Great Depression *and* the reces-sion of 2008 combined. A job is more than a way to support oneself and one's loved ones. As the *New York Times* summed up the impact, a job is "an identity, a civic stabilizer, a future builder."[45]

The economy shrank. Small businesses, such as restaurants, bars, and retail stores, closed at a record pace. In New York City, one-third of all small businesses closed just between March and early August 2020.[46]

The impact of economic collapse on individuals and families proved devastating. During 2020, six to eight million additional Americans fell into poverty (an annual income below $28,170 for a family of four) or deep poverty (an annual income of less than $14,581 for a family of four). By September more than one in five American children were living in households that qualified as poor under federal guidelines. These figures translate into concrete hardships: "food insufficiency, missed/delayed rent payments, and frequent anxiety," as well as lack of utilities, and well-founded fear of eviction.[47]

Absent federal protections as many as thirty to forty million people risked eviction by the end of 2020. Researchers found that renters with children faced the highest risk of eviction, and about 80 percent of those at risk of eviction were Black or Latinx, the same groups whose members were at greatest risk of contracting COVID-19.[48]

The technically poor were not alone in their suffering; a large proportion of households with incomes up to $100,000 reported "serious financial problems." A national survey conducted by NPR, the Robert Wood Johnson Foundation, and the Harvard T. H. Chan School of Public Health in July and August 2020 found that 46 percent of all households reported "serious financial problems" including lost jobs, reduced wages, or loss of a business they owned, and depletion of savings. About one in five households reported that they either could not pay, or anticipated problems paying, their credit card bills, loans, mortgage, or rent, with the highest concentration of distress again falling on Black and Latinx households.[49]

Hunger also skyrocketed. Nearly thirty million Americans (almost one in ten) lacked sufficient food. Feeding America, a coalition of food pantries, reported a 56 percent increase in distributions during the third quarter of 2020 compared to the prior year. Some 40 percent of the recipients had never turned to a food bank prior to the pandemic. Nightly news reveals miles-long lines of cars holding families waiting for a food package.[50]

In assessing these different kinds of harm, it is obviously difficult to disentangle the impact of Trump's lies from the impact of his cavalier approach to the public health crisis, his lack of a plan, and his attempt to foist responsibility off to the governors. Right now, I cannot assign a percentage of the fault to Trump's dishonesty as compared to his reckless policies, though perhaps someday social scientists will be able to come up with a number. What is clear is that some portion of the death and hardship the United States experienced must surely be attributed to President Trump's dishonesty about every aspect of the pandemic. In February 2021, a *Lancet* commission reported that some 40 percent of the COVID-19 deaths in the United States could have been avoided by using nonmedical interventions (like masks and social distancing) of the sort Trump discouraged.[51]

Regardless of the precise amount of blame that Trump bears, his mendacity made a disaster he did not cause many times worse than it had to be. As 2020 drew to a close, with new cases and daily deaths rising dramatically, PolitiFact gave "Coronavirus downplay and denial" the Lie of the Year Award: "not just damaging, but deadly." Although Trump shared the award with others, PolitiFact called him "the conductor, if not the composer," of a "symphony of counter-narrative."[52]

When you read this book, you will know more than I can as the book goes to press about how the pandemic unfolded after Trump left office. But the glimmer of hope for the future in the promise of vaccination and a change of government does not diminish Trump's culpability for intentionally misleading the country about the grave risks COVID-19 posed and about how we should or should not strive to protect ourselves.

What if there had been a way to cut the president's lies short months before he left office?

CHAPTER 6

The President Works for Us

"Total honesty is what we as citizens deserve from our president," declared First Lady Melania Trump without a trace of irony, addressing the Republican Convention virtually from the White House Rose Garden on August 25, 2020.[1] She was right, although no president is likely to achieve "total" honesty, least of all her truth-challenged husband. Still, Donald Trump's brazen contempt for truth extended the tail of the bell curve of presidential lies so far to the right (meaning the most lies per day, not the political leanings of the liar) that the preservation of democracy itself calls out for some means of ensuring we never see his like in the Oval Office again.

This chapter returns to the momentous question presented on the opening page of this book: What can we do, consistent with the First Amendment, to stop a president who endangers our very lives and our democracy by lying incessantly?

My analysis of the apparently insurmountable constitutional impediments to regulating factual falsehoods may have left readers in despair, but the First Amendment is not the problem when it comes to mendacious presidents. A constitutional solution exists, if there is a political will to invoke it.

Former President Trump's second impeachment trial squarely presented the issue of whether the First Amendment inoculates all of a president's expression from accountability, as his lawyers essentially claimed. The legal question of how a president's freedom of expression compares to the expressive rights of others—whether it is greater, the same, or less—remains unresolved because it was not answered during that proceeding. Trump's lawyers got it backwards, as I will demonstrate.

This chapter repudiates any claim that the First Amendment provides cover for a president who persists in spreading material factual falsehoods. The next chapter considers the constitutional steps that could theoretically be used to implement my proposal, as well as the serious impediments to effectuating it under current political conditions.

Skeptics may wonder whether I am like the generals who are said to always be fighting the last war. Of course, we need to remain alert to risks that remain unimaginable. But since the previously unimaginable became reality during the Trump administration, we must anticipate the risk that we will have another president who is tempted to spread bald-faced lies. We should be prepared with an analytically sound response that recognizes the power of words even when they are not accompanied by the illicit or suspect actions that so frequently surrounded Trump's falsehoods.

To some extent, my quest may be quixotic. For the moment, I urge readers to consider it an opening gambit for a longer and broader dialogue.

The many respected pundits and scholars from other disciplines who have figuratively screamed from the rooftops that pervasive, bold, repeated lies are the authoritarian ruler's best friend and a step toward decimating meaningful democracy have not had to take the First Amendment into account. They used different lenses. As a First Amendment scholar, I must ask whether the Speech Clause permits regulation of presidential deception and, if so, how?

No one, not even a president, has a constitutional "right to lie." As I have shown, no court or even a single justice has ever gone so far as to recognize such a right under the First Amendment. To say that lies are not devoid of constitutional protection is a far cry from imputing an affirmative right to fabricate no matter what the harm to others or the motive.

The bottom line in *United States* v. *Alvarez* was clear if not fully formulated: Under some circumstances not yet defined, the government may be able to criminalize lies without violating the First Amendment. More specifically, before the government can punish factual falsehoods it must show a level of harm to others or unwarranted benefit to the speaker that satisfies the applicable standard of review (whatever that turns out to be). Perhaps that is not as pellucid as we might hope, but it is a far cry from an unrestricted right to promote factual falsehoods.

I will argue—perhaps counterintuitively—that presidents should be held to a higher standard of truthfulness than can be imposed on the population at large or on mere candidates for public office.

I rely on two broader legal justifications for this proposition.

The first involves harm. A president's bald-faced lies have unparalleled potential to cause harm, creating a compelling interest in stopping the flow of dangerous mendacity. I have amply demonstrated the harms that flowed from Trump's lies about COVID-19, examined in the last chapter, and the existential threat to democracy posed by his lies about the 2020 election, described in Chapter 1. If those examples do not meet the standard floated in *Alvarez*—the "something more" to which Justice Kennedy alluded—it is hard to imagine what level of harm would be sufficient to override any First Amendment claim to a right to lie.

Second, a theoretical wrinkle within the Speech Clause opens the door to regulating presidential lies without infringing on a president's freedom of expression. A special doctrine allows the government to censor and punish a great deal of expression by public employees. It offers a rationale for restricting mendacious presidents and other high officials subject to congressional oversight.

The Speaker's Posture

The insight that the president is a public servant, albeit a very highly placed one, holds the key to mandating that presidents refrain from engaging in a pattern of verifiable factual falsehoods. The posture of a president's speech matters. Initially, we must determine whether the president speaks as the government, as a government employee, or as an individual.

Government Speech

The government as an entity (federal, state, or local) often "speaks." Government agencies select, explain, and publicize policies. The state's expressive functions include formulating curricular requirements for schools, running public media outlets like state university radio stations, and issuing informational pamphlets and website content prepared by government agencies. The government cannot do its job in these contexts without choosing content and viewpoint—preferences that would violate the Constitution if the state imposed them on private citizens or institutions.

When the government speaks, it has speech rights just like you or me. The government has virtually unlimited discretion to promote any viewpoint it chooses as if it were an individual engaging in protected expression. However, when the executive branch tells official lies that can be disproven, congressional oversight or voters may hold it accountable.

That may be easier said than done. It can be exceptionally difficult to prove that the executive branch is spreading falsehoods, especially when deception touches on matters of national security. (Since the early days of the Republic, the executive branch has asserted that some executive functions, such as diplomacy, require a period of secrecy in order to be effective, and the Supreme Court agrees.) If the government controls all of the evidence that disproves its factually false statements, it may be impossible for journalists, researchers, and even congressional oversight committees to discover the deception, much less prove it. Freedom of Information Act requests are intended as a remedy, but the government too often refuses to release documents, slow tracks requests, or redacts material.

Is the President the Government?

President Trump, his attorney general William Barr, and their cronies relied on the unitary executive theory in claiming almost limitless powers for the president. The view that the president has quasi-monarchical authority traces its roots to President Nixon, who famously asserted in a 1977 interview, "When the President does it, that means that it is not illegal."[2] Although Nixon's contention flew in the face of the principle that no person is above the law in our democracy, his broad premise gained adherents in the intervening decades.

The Trump presidency adopted an extreme posture regarding presidential power. Harvard law professor Alan Dershowitz, defending President Trump at his first impeachment trial in 2020, stunned constitutional experts when he claimed: "If a President does something which he believes will help him get elected—in the public interest—that cannot be the kind of quid pro quo that results in impeachment." Trump himself repeatedly and falsely proclaimed, "I have an Article 2 [in the Constitution], where I have the right to do whatever I want as President." According to Miles Taylor, who resigned as chief of staff in the Department of Homeland Security during Trump's term, Trump swatted off efforts to educate him about the constitutional limits on the president, insisting he had "magical authorities."[3]

In reality, by enumerating specific presidential powers, Article II of the Constitution limits what the president may do, just as the assignment of particular powers to Congress under Article I expressly removes those powers from the president. When Trump professed unlimited powers under Article II he was either telling a bald-faced lie or revealing his lack of minimal understanding. If Trump believed he had magical authorities, he was delusional. In that case, the statement, while terrifying, would not meet the legal definition of a verifiable falsehood.

Trump's magical thinking might satisfy other definitions of lying. Responding to the difficulty of establishing any liar's intent, Eric Alterman argued in *Lying in State*, published shortly before the 2020 election, that we need a much more expansive definition to confront presidential lies. Alterman posits that a presidential lie "takes place when the president or someone with the authority to speak for the president seeks to purposefully mislead the country about a matter of political significance."[4]

Alterman's clarion call denounces a political culture that rewards lies and false equivalency in the media. He argues we must circumvent the intent requirement found in Augustinian philosophy and legal rules in order to account for the true range of deception. To Alterman, "the only significant criterion is whether the deception itself, however operationally undertaken, is purposeful" and concerns a matter of political significance. Unlike current law (which requires proof of an intent to deceive), Alterman's definition might reach nearly all of Trump's falsehoods, including those based on magical thinking and on his reported inability to distinguish truth from falsehood.[5]

It matters a great deal whether the president speaks as the government or as an individual, because as an individual who works for the government the president arguably has less First Amendment protections than I do as a tenured professor or than any person who does not work for local, state, or federal government. When presidents address the nation, talk to the press, or post on social media, they do not necessarily speak as "the government." They often speak only as individuals. Even then, they are individuals who work for the government, a fact that has constitutional significance, as I will explain. (The calculation may well be different when presidents act as heads of state rather than chief executives—for example, when they meet officially with other heads of state or pardon the Thanksgiving turkey.)

When presidents speak as individuals, no matter how powerful, their leeway to choose what they say and how they say it, including whether to speak truthfully or not, can and should be limited. Doing so would not violate the First Amendment rights of presidents because they work for the federal government and, ultimately, for the American people.

The Limited Speech Rights of Employees

Neither public nor private employers are required to respect the free speech of their employees. Everyone who works for someone else, whether in the private or public sector, risks severe repercussions, including dismissal, based on what they say. But private and public employers operate under different legal regimes.

Private Employers and Employee Speech

The Speech Clause does not apply to private employers because they are not the state. The First Amendment only limits state action, that is, action by any level of government. Unless labor agreements or similar provisions expressly protect workers' speech rights, private employers are free to discipline and fire employees for what they say.

That is why football teams were able to fire or discipline football players led by Colin Kaepernick, who took the knee to protest police brutality toward Black people while the national anthem played starting in 2016. Sidelining protesting players may not be good policy, but it does not violate the Constitution. Policy and marketing concerns finally led the National Football League to allow player protests starting in 2020 in response to renewed national discussions about police brutality and race relations. The league and team owners had full discretion to make either decision.

Private employers do not violate any laws when they fire workers for what the workers say inside or outside the workplace, in a bar, or on social media if the employer or others find the speech offensive, if it is thought to reflect badly on the company, or for any reason at all. Recall utility company employee Melissa Campbell, who reported Xavier Alvarez to the FBI? Fired by her private employer. You may not remember Juli Briskman's name, but you probably remember what she did—she is the woman on the bicycle who displayed her middle finger to President Trump's motorcade early in his first term. After she briefly became the heroine of a large swath of social media, her employer, Akima, a federal government contractor, fired her. Although no constitutional remedy was available to Briskman, her case has a silver lining. The citizens of Loudoun County, Virginia, elected her to the county Board of Supervisors on November 5, 2019.

Government Employees

More surprising to many, First Amendment protections against government censorship are unavailable to people who work for the government, also known as "public employees." In contrast to the rest of us, who the government generally cannot punish for what we say, when public employees speak about topics related to their jobs, the Speech Clause does not protect them from retaliation by the government in its stance as their employer.

Although public employees do not relinquish all their speech rights by accepting government positions, those rights are generally restricted to the rights they would "enjoy as citizens to comment on matters of public interest."[6] That definition is not as broad as it sounds. Most of us do not need to address matters of public interest to avail ourselves of free expression. Residents of the United States enjoy constitutional protection when they speak out about matters that are of no interest at all to anyone but themselves regardless of how ill-informed, frivolous, or obnoxious their expression may be.

The public employee speech doctrine is susceptible to criticism for silencing a great deal of speech in settings that could benefit from a freer exchange of ideas. (As a legal scholar I have voiced some of those concerns elsewhere.)[7] As an attorney, however, I take the doctrine, the law of the land, as I find it and base my approach to tackling presidential mendacity on it.

Over fifty years ago in *Pickering* v. *Board of Education*, the Supreme Court crafted a special standard to govern expression by public employees. When public employees claim that the state penalized them in the workplace for expression the Speech Clause should have protected, courts apply the rules *Pickering* established.[8]

Public employees who claim unlawful retaliation for protected speech must satisfy two preconditions before a court will consider whether their governmental employer violated their speech rights. At the outset, the court will ask whether they spoke as private citizens and whether they addressed the public about a matter of public concern. If the answer to either question is no, the case will be dismissed. Then the employee has no right to seek relief in court, and the adverse employment decision remains in place. If, and only if, the answer to both questions is yes, employees may present evidence to a court that the First Amendment protects their expression.

The threshold requirement that government workers must convince a judge that they speak as private citizens poses a very high hurdle when the expression is related in any way to the scope of the worker's employment. If any nexus is found between the speech and the employee's duties, the government can restrict employee expression just as much as any private employer can.

Government workers' claims do not usually survive these threshold questions, but when they do, the court does not apply strict scrutiny. Instead, it uses *Pickering*'s balancing test, which is much easier for the state to satisfy. The court weighs the worker's speech rights against the government's asserted interest as an employer. The employer's interests may include promoting efficiency, preserving the agency's public reputation, or institutional harmony—none of which would pass muster as a compelling interest under strict scrutiny. In the rare event that the case moves forward to trial after that analysis, the state has a number of additional opportunities to rebut the worker's First Amendment claims.

Public employee speech embraces a vast scope: all expression made "pursuant to professional duties."[9] Subjects fall within the scope of employment for public employees if, for example, employees learned information in the course of their jobs or spoke about their workplaces; expressed views to a work colleague or supervisor, including complaints about irregularities; testified about facts related to their work; or said something in public that could reflect badly on their office or disrupt its efficiency.

In 2006 the Supreme Court clarified this standard in *Garcetti* v. *Ceballos*. Ceballos, a Los Angeles County supervising deputy district attorney working in Pomona, California, alleged that his supervisors retaliated against him after he wrote an office memo urging the office to drop a criminal prosecution because the search warrant application was flawed. His superiors disagreed. Ceballos defied them by testifying pursuant to a subpoena on the defendant's behalf about the warrant's defects. The Supreme Court held that Ceballos's memo and testimony lacked First Amendment protections because both flowed from his professional duties. It was irrelevant that Ceballos directly contradicted what his superiors wanted him to say—his expression remained within the scope of his work.[10]

The eminent conservative jurist Frank Easterbrook explained the core takeaway from *Ceballos* in 2020. The First Amendment has no bearing on "how public employers manage their workforces," he wrote, "even when that management involves telling others what to say or avoid saying. Words said, or omitted, as part of official duties" are subject to the applicable state law. It is as if the First Amendment did not exist if those words fall "within the scope" of the worker's duties.[11]

The saga of Army Lieutenant Colonel Alexander Vindman, who testified during the 2020 House of Representatives impeachment hearings on President Trump, aptly illustrates the risks truth-tellers take given the lack of protection for public employee speech. A staff member at the National Security Council (NSC), Colonel Vindman had been asked to listen in real time to the July 25, 2019 telephone call between Trump and Ukrainian President Volodymyr Zelensky—the "do us a favor" call in which Trump tried to extort a foreign leader to help him undermine former Vice President Joe Biden, his presumptive Democratic challenger. That conversation was the basis for one of the counts in Trump's first impeachment.

After the Republican majority in the Senate declined to call any witnesses at the trial, and failed to convict the president, Colonel Vindman was unceremoniously removed from his position at the NSC. So was his twin brother, Army Lieutenant Colonel Yevgeny Vindman, a lawyer detailed to the NSC who had not played any role in the impeachment proceedings. Colonel Alexander Vindman's pending promotion did not move forward. His military career was essentially over. A few months later Colonel Vindman retired under pressure, protesting "a campaign of bullying, intimidation and retaliation."[12]

It is painful to recall the colonel reassuring his father on national television during his sworn testimony that the United States was not the Soviet Union, which the family had fled: "Do not worry, I will be fine for telling the truth."[13] Even if he had not been in uniform, the First Amendment would not have protected Colonel Alexander Vindman. He was a public employee, testifying about information he acquired in the course of his employment. Only federal whistleblower protection might have safeguarded either of the Vindmans.

Of course, some public employees who speak out are hardly heroes. Consider Arthur Love IV, who was fired by the state of Maryland for his social media posts. Love, the deputy director of the Governor's Office of Community Initiatives, oversaw the state's Commission on African American

History and Culture. After seventeen-year-old Kyle Rittenhouse was charged with killing two Black Lives Matter protesters and wounding another in Kenosha, Wisconsin, Love supported Rittenhouse on Facebook. Rittenhouse's victims were protesting police violence, specifically the recent shooting of Jacob Blake, a Black man, by police officers who shot him in the back seven times, leaving Blake paralyzed. Rittenhouse, a White youth, had used an AR-15 rifle, a lightweight semiautomatic gun that is a weapon of choice in mass shootings. Maryland discharged the inaptly named Love because his posts supporting Rittenhouse and stating that Rittenhouse "genuinely seems like a good person" were "inconsistent with the mission and core values" of his agency, which promoted African American culture.[14]

The government's wide discretion to fire employees for speech on their own time occasionally encounters modest limitations. The narrowness of those limitations clarifies the extensive reach of the public employee speech doctrine.

In *United States* v. *National Treasury Employees Union* (*"Treasury Employees"*), decided in 1995, the Supreme Court overturned the section of a federal statute that barred nearly 1.7 million lower-level employees of the executive branch from accepting honoraria or other compensation for writing or speaking about any topic—including subjects that had no relationship to their employment. The court easily concluded that the ban impermissibly chilled a great deal of speech that public employees might engage in as private citizens. Prohibiting speakers from receiving even modest remuneration discouraged them from writing articles, preparing lectures, and similar activities outside of work hours.

Treasury Employees underscores how far removed the speech must be from the speaker's duties to satisfy *Pickering*'s "private citizen" requirement. The federal employees who brought the case included a postal service mail handler who had lectured on the Quaker religion; an aerospace engineer at the Goddard Space Flight Center who had lectured on Black history; a Food and Drug Administration microbiologist who reviewed dance performances; and a tax examiner for the Internal Revenue Service who published articles about the environment.

The court worried about the cultural losses that might result from this sort of far-reaching prior restraint. "Federal employees," like Nathaniel Hawthorne and Herman Melville, both of whom worked for the Customs Service, "who write for publication in their spare time," the court observed, "have made significant contributions to the marketplace of ideas." They would have been discouraged from writing if they could not profit from their creations, depriving society of great works of art.[15]

This line of authority provides important support for my approach to regulating presidential lies. As an employer, the government has complete discretion to fire almost every worker who engages in disfavored speech—whether at work, outside work, on social media, or at a bar—if that expression can be linked to the employee's workplace or duties.

Presidents as Public Employees

Presidents work for us: "we the people." That much should be incontrovertible.

Classifying Presidents

No court appears to have considered whether—as a general matter—a president is a public employee, but the 1982 opinion in *Nixon* v. *Fitzgerald* provides guidance. A. Ernest Fitzgerald's job in the Department of the Air Force was eliminated after he delivered truthful but embarrassing testimony to a congressional committee. President Richard M. Nixon personally approved the controversial dismissal buried in a reorganization. Fitzgerald sued him, alleging retribution for his testimony.

When the case reached the Supreme Court, the question of whether the president was immune to civil suit for his official acts turned on the meaning of a federal statute. The act defined a group of executive department officials whom individuals could sue for harms caused by their official acts. The court held that President Nixon had absolute immunity from a civil suit by an aggrieved former government employee—but only because Congress had not included the president in the category of officials rendered subject to private lawsuits.

No constitutional question was presented. Neither the president's constitutional status as a government employee nor the scope of his duties was before the court. Had Congress included the president among the employees who could be sued, the court implied, it would have respected that legislative decision. In other words, the holding does not support the assertion that there is any constitutional bar to categorizing the president as a public employee.[16]

Despite the lack of legal authority, during Trump's second impeachment trial his attorneys argued that *no* elected official (not just the president) can be classified as a public employee for any purpose. They relied on two other Supreme Court cases for this proposition, neither of which stands for the principle they put forward: *Wood* v. *Georgia*, decided in 1962, and *Bond* v. *Floyd*, decided in 1966.

Both cases were decided before the court formalized the public employee speech doctrine in *Pickering* in 1968. There was no reason for the court to consider whether elected officials were distinguishable from civil servants and other appointees with respect to speech rights. Moreover, neither *Wood* nor *Bond* implicates the question whether an elected official is a public employee.

In *Wood*, the court agreed with an elected sheriff who argued that his First Amendment rights were violated when a trial judge held him in contempt for public statements challenging a grand jury proceeding relating to Black voters. But the sheriff did not mention his public office when he spoke out about this charged political topic. The court expressly stated that Wood's position as sheriff had not been used to provide "any basis for curtailing his right of free speech," that it was not "significant as to his news releases," and that the speech did not interfere with either "his duties as sheriff" or "the administration of justice."[17] The opinion never stated that the sheriff was not a public employee for First Amendment purposes.

Bond v. *Floyd* does not address the public employee status of elected officials either. The case involved the limits of legislative self-governance that interfered with speech rights. The Georgia House of Representatives refused to seat the duly elected delegate from a majority-Black district—civil rights leader Julian Bond. It considered him ineligible to take the loyalty oath required at the swearing-in based on his articulated, fully protected political opposition to war and his commitment to racial activism.

The court held that the legislature violated Bond's First Amendment rights by penalizing speech that would be protected for a "private citizen" based on its standards of *loyalty*. The exclusion was, the court held, based entirely on Bond's political views, which required "the widest latitude."[18]

The court did not discuss potential distinctions between appointed and elected officials in either *Bond* or *Wood*. Equally important, legislators are distinguishable from those elected to fulfill executive functions because discipline of legislators is entrusted to the legislative body, which the Constitution also charges with oversight of the federal executive branch.

In light of this doctrinal history, no apparent analytical justification mandates exempting presidents from the legal constraints that apply to other public servants who perform executive functions.

Everything Presidents Say Is Related to Their Job

The factors used to decide whether speech is related to a public employee's job establish that when presidents communicate they almost always speak as public employees. There is almost nothing a president could address during his or her term in office that can be disconnected from the Executive Office of the President. By its very nature, the presidency is a year-round 24/7 job. It spans nearly infinite aspects of life.

Beyond the broad substantive scope of the president's employment, the indicia of presidential office are always visible. Security details, staff, and reporters surround presidents all the time. The locales where presidents most often speak demonstrate that they speak as public employees: whether from the Oval Office, the Rose Garden, *Air Force One*, or Camp David. This remains true in any physical space where presidents are accompanied by Secret Service protection—that is, everywhere a president goes, including a vacation rental, private home, international venue, or golf club.

Even when presidents post impetuously on social media, their identity as POTUS remains transcendent. In 2017 and again in 2018, the Department of Justice told federal courts that Trump's tweets from the POTUS account were "official statements" of the president and of government policy.[19]

In 2020, the Court of Appeals for the Second Circuit roundly rejected Trump's claim that his personal Twitter account could be delinked from his status as president. Tweets from that account, the court reasoned, must remain open to the public because they were used to announce policy, "published by a public official clothed with the authority of the state using social media as a tool of governance." Those tweets were issued "in his capacity as the nation's chief executive and Commander-in-Chief."[20]

Social media sites proclaimed the official nature of a president's postings by giving them special treatment. For example, during the summer of 2020 Facebook announced that it would not remove material posted by the president even if the posts violated its policies and would have been removed had anyone else shared them. It adhered to that policy until Trump's communications grew ever more outrageous and endangered people.

Great privilege and great power come at the cost of bright lines between the personal and the public. That assumption is baked into the First Amendment limitations the Supreme Court has placed on defamation recovery by public figures, discussed in Chapter 3. No public figure in the world is more ubiquitous than the president of the United States.

Arguably, there may be narrow exceptions to the notion that presidents always speak as public employees. Presidents who elect to share what are clearly labeled their own personal religious beliefs, for example, should be treated as expressing their individual views. If they were speaking in an official capacity, their statements might give rise to a claim under the Establishment Clause.

Perhaps a president's statements about immediate family members or about the president's intimate life (if not under oath) could qualify as personal. Announcements about the birth of a child, where his or her children will attend school, or summer vacation plans could be insufficiently tied to the vast scope of presidential employment to be rendered the speech of a private citizen. I have my doubts.

During the summer of 2020 when reporters asked whether President Trump's son would attend his elite private school in person or online in the fall, the answer held political significance. The president was exhorting schools to open and parents to send their children (at serious risk of illness and death). Would he be taking comparable risks for his son and family?

The mainstream press once refrained from publicizing intimate details of a president's life: Warren Harding's long-term extramarital relationships and the existence of a daughter born outside of marriage; Franklin Roosevelt's relationship with his longtime secretary Marguerite "Missy" LeHand; Dwight D. Eisenhower's reputed affair with his woman driver; and John F. Kennedy's escapades, some of them on the White House grounds.

Any bright line between a president's intimate life and his official one was at least partially eviscerated during the Clinton administration. No behavior by the president, before or after his term in office, remained out of bounds, especially after Independent Counsel Kenneth Starr's lengthy published report shared intimate facts in excruciating detail. Public discussions increasingly turned on personal character and inherent fitness for office. Critiques were not limited to acts related to presidential responsibilities.

When a president lies to the public about his intimate life, however smarmy, the falsehood is arguably so divorced from the scope of his duties as to be the protected speech of a private citizen, albeit a citizen who is constantly under a spotlight.

But in September 2020 the Department of Justice abandoned the ability to make that claim when it argued in federal court that presidential statements denying sexual crimes that allegedly occurred years earlier were part of the president's job. The Department of Justice sought to substitute the United States as the defendant in lieu of Donald J. Trump, who had been sued for defamation by E. Jean Carroll.

In 2019, anticipating imminent publication of a book in which Carroll alleged that Trump had raped her in the 1990s in a luxury Manhattan department store, President Trump denied Carroll's charges. He called her a liar, and gratuitously added that he could not have raped her because, he said, "she's not my type." The statute of limitations had long since passed, so the rape could not be prosecuted. Carroll could only vindicate the truthfulness of her accusation by suing Trump for defamation, which she did in New York state court.

Many months later, with Trump facing an order to provide a DNA sample, the Department of Justice moved to intervene, reportedly at Trump's prodding. If the court granted the motion, the US government would be substituted for Trump as the defendant. The statute on which the government relied in seeking to become the defendant allows individuals to sue the federal government itself for torts committed by its employees in the scope of their employment (such as damage from a car accident en route to inspect a waste site).

Critically, the terms of the statute blocked the Carroll lawsuit from proceeding. The statute expressly withholds the government's consent to being sued for *defamation* based on something an employee said. Federal courts are required to dismiss any defamation case in which the United States becomes the defendant.

Applying that policy to Carroll's lawsuit, the Department of Justice certified (institutionally swore) that President Trump "was acting within the scope of his office or employment" when he defamed Carroll. It ignored the fact that the president was not a government employee when the alleged underlying crime occurred. He was a private citizen, and the alleged rape took place decades before he had ever held public office.[21]

As I paraphrase it, the department's claim reduces to "the president's job includes defaming private citizens about matters that have no relation to public policy or decision making."

That laughable posture constitutes an enormous concession when applied to my argument. The Trump administration waived the ability to claim that *any* presidential statement at all is disconnected from the president's official duties. Even if the department's argument on Trump's behalf does not bind future presidents, my argument would not be seriously diminished by a future administration's disavowal of the preposterous claim that Trump's defamatory speech was part of his job.

Trump was stymied. The federal district court refused to substitute the United States for Trump because the president did not fit within the detailed statutory definition of an "employee of the Government." The court's analysis of the particular statute on which the department relied does not affect my broader conceptual argument that the president is a public employee who works for the citizens.[22]

Defining Presidential Lies for Constitutional Purposes

I propose that presidents should be subject to extreme penalties for a continuing pattern of material verifiable falsehoods that harm the body politic or the well-being of the American people. The penalties I have in mind—described further in the next chapter—are based on the structure of constitutional governance, specifically the separation of powers. None of the argument that follows is intended to justify extending criminal prosecution or the availability of civil damages beyond what the applicable law and the Speech Clause already permit.

It is no easy matter to define the scope of the presidential lies that might be subject to discipline. Even when common sense indicates that a speaker intends to deceive, agreement on whether a statement fits the legal definition of a lie may prove elusive, as the case of Wisconsin justice Michael Gableman illustrated, especially if partisan politics is in play.

With that reservation in mind, it is imperative to define the falsehoods I have in mind as clearly as possible. Although the First Amendment does not apply to government employees, the Speech Clause doctrine offers guidance about how to formulate a cautious definition of "presidential lies." The definition should be neither too broad nor too narrow, and should be carefully tailored to prevent chilling too much expression that the First Amendment would protect outside the realm of employee speech.

For exploratory purposes, presidential lies are comprised of a continuing pattern of material verifiable falsehoods (what I have been referring to as "bald-faced" lies) that are likely to significantly harm the body politic. This standard has much in common with Eric Alterman's "purposeful" misleading statement "about a matter of political significance," but I add constitutional safeguards, among them verifiability, materiality, and a sustained pattern of falsehood.[23]

I emphasize bald-faced lies because proving their falsity would be relatively straightforward. In theory, when the facts that expose the falsehoods are a matter of public record, no ambiguity should remain for a president to hide behind. Concededly, in a country that appears to be divided over the very nature of established facts, in which many prefer what Trump's Senior Counselor Kellyanne Conway called "alternative facts," even that elemental level of agreement may prove unattainable.

My proposal is limited to "material" falsehoods. Materiality is a basic building block of both civil and criminal law. A false material statement to the government has a "natural tendency to influence, or [be] capable of influencing," a decision or, in the case of a government agency, the agency's general functioning.[24] When a statement has the potential to influence an outcome there is no need to prove that the statement actually affected what happened in order to establish materiality. Although materiality can be hotly contested, it is a familiar enough construct in courtrooms to be manageable in any type of formal inquiry.

There should be a sustained pattern of falsehoods, not a one-off. The pattern may consist of falsehoods about one topic, such as a baseless attack on election results. Or it might be a pattern of lies about "virtually all topics," as law professor Frank O. Bowman III postulated when he asked "whether numerous unrelated falsehoods, none of which standing alone, can be aggregated into an offense meriting removal from office." Bowman suggests that a president's *"pervasive"* lies undermine every branch of government as well as foreign relations but stops short of endorsing an effort to control the damage in light of the definitional and political obstacles.[25] I press further, though I do not claim to have resolved all of the potential issues.

A continuing pattern or a finding of pervasiveness critically protects a president from being subjected to a "gotcha" moment by a Congress lying in wait. Requiring a pattern of lies offers the president a safety valve. As an additional protection I propose that the liar may be relieved of accountability by expressly retracting the falsehood after being confronted with verifiable facts that expose the lie for what it is, and by refraining from repeating the falsehood.

This approach would result in a more forgiving standard than applies in defamation or to the average public employee. Defamatory speakers remain accountable for a single false statement because the lie is in circulation. Victims who sue may be seeking a retraction, but issuing one does not result in a clean slate. Public employees who lose their jobs as a result of unprotected speech may have spoken only once, may have reached almost no one with their speech, and are unprotected even if they lacked any harmful intent.

Proof of recklessness or intent plays no part where the inhibitions on speech rights of public employees are concerned, and proving intent should not be necessary when it comes to presidential lies. The usual due process concerns are muted in the absence of criminal or civil liability. What is more, to the extent that my proposal would allow a president to escape discipline by retracting a lie upon being confronted with the verifiable facts, refusal to retract or choosing to continue the lie should establish intent without further inquiry. Intent might remain problematic in cases where a president is impervious to truth, as in a president who continues to insist the moon is made of blue cheese and a man lives there. Relying on public employee speech doctrine would relieve us of any need to prove that such a president knew he or she was lying.

Exceptions to my working definition of presidential lies may be necessary, for example, to allow the president to preserve the confidentiality of compelling, narrowly defined national security interests. Such interests could include, among other things, the existence, location, or movement of troops or machinery of war; the undetected use of cyber-warfare by the United States; the existence or identity of intelligence assets; or negotiations with foreign governments, to the extent secrecy is a precondition for discussions. These carve-outs would be subject to the understanding that the executive branch would continue to provide truthful disclosure to a select group of congressional leaders with the highest level of security clearance. There is no guarantee. We know all too well that such deference is subject to abuse, as when successive administrations secretly expanded the war in Southeast Asia during the 1960s, and when President George W. Bush initiated a war in Iraq based on nonexistent weapons of mass destruction.

Presidential lies pollute the national discourse and decimate rational decision making even when those lies are perfectly legal for anyone else to utter. The falsehoods I envision constraining would not have to be voiced under oath or in an official pronouncement, although falsehoods in either of those settings would count as presidential lies. The deception could be floated in any setting, as long as it was addressed to the public.

Falsehoods come in a wide variety of forms, some of which are easier to pin down than others. Before he was president, Trump prided himself on his skillful skirting of responsibility through what he called "truthful hyperbole" in *The Art of the Deal*, a contradiction in terms. In public life he commonly stepped back from outrageous assertions by labeling them "jokes."

I emphasize bald-faced lies because they presumably provide less room for quibbling over ambiguities, knowledge, and intent, especially if the verifiable facts are a matter of public record. Although my definition would fail to reach many presidential deceptions that take the form of intentional distortion, prevarication, or even bullshit, it offers a path forward.

CHAPTER 7

Lies Matter

I t may seem as if nothing can be done to stop mendacious presidents regardless of how dangerous their lies or what constitutional theory one
proposes. Readers may feel helpless in the wake of the Senate's largely
partisan decision to acquit President Trump in both of his impeachment
trials, epistemic tribalism, and raw pursuit of partisan power by one political party, combined with rampant disinformation and outright attacks on
democracy.

But four years of a Trump presidency heightened the urgency of holding
presidents to account for the destructive factual falsehoods I defined in
the last chapter as presidential lies. That urgency became even starker
when Trump's lawyers argued in his second impeachment trial that presidents have "enhanced free speech rights" as elected officials to say whatever
they want.[1]

In this closing chapter I press further to examine the status of a president's expressive rights in the face of congressional scrutiny, and what steps
Congress could take to discipline presidential lies relying on its general
oversight responsibilities as enhanced by public employee speech doctrine.

Starkly put, does a president have a constitutional right to lie? If, as
United States v. *Alvarez* strongly suggests, some lies will prove so harmful
that the government may regulate them without offending the Speech
Clause, surely Trump's lies about COVID-19 and the 2020 election results
cross that threshold. If they do not, it seems no level of falsehood would.

The chapter begins by highlighting the centrality of presidential deceit
in the Nixon and Clinton impeachments, neither of which considered a potential free speech defense. Then I analyze the congressional oversight role. I
consider how invocation of the public employee speech doctrine as applied

to a president could be used to fortify oversight, explain why Congress is uniquely positioned to discipline presidential lies, and explore a range of escalating remedies Congress could put into play. Finally, I consider the role of lies and the misplaced First Amendment defense in Trump's second impeachment and trial.

Impeachment: The Constitutional Failsafe

The Constitution assigns to Congress the grave responsibility of overseeing the president, up to and including impeachment, trial, and removal from office. The grounds for impeachment are stated succinctly. Article II, Section 4 of the Constitution gives Congress sole authority over impeachments of federal officials for "Treason, Bribery or other high Crimes and Misdemeanors."

The Role of Presidential Lies in Past Impeachments

The role presidential lies played in modern presidential impeachment proceedings has been critical to my inquiry into the relationship between free speech and public lies. All three of the presidents who have been impeached or threatened with imminent impeachment since Reconstruction lied to the American public.

Those lies to the public became central to the impeachment hearings and proceedings that followed. None of the proceedings relied in any way on the president's status as a government employee, though all were decided after *Pickering* v. *Board of Education* limited the speech rights of public employees in 1968. The first two (involving Presidents Nixon and Clinton) skirted the question of whether the First Amendment shelters mendacious presidents, while the third (President Trump's second impeachment) left the issue unresolved.

When Congress considered the Nixon and Clinton cases, it never asked what made lying to the public an impeachable offense. It seemed to go without saying that lying is dishonorable; it besmirches the presidency. Congress has never squarely considered whether factual falsehoods, without more, could amount to an impeachable offense. Nor has it confronted a corollary question: To what extent does the Speech Clause protect presidential expression?

Perhaps the original rationale for impeachment was the rather quaint and yet inspiring notion of holding officials to high standards of integrity and probity in their public life. The late constitutional scholar Charles Black, discussing the "kinds" of violations impeachment is intended to address, included those "which are plainly wrong in themselves to a person of honor, or to a good citizen."[2] In the founders' world, gentlemen in public office would readily recognize a person of honor. He might be a scoundrel in his intimate life (like Alexander Hamilton or Thomas Jefferson), but he would not be a liar.

Michael Gerhardt, author of a leading contemporary treatise on impeachment, echoes Black's conclusion. Abuses against the state are impeachable because they subvert the "public trust." The offender loses "the confidence of the people and, consequently, [he or she] must forfeit the privilege of holding at least his or her present office."[3]

In the cases involving Nixon and Clinton, lies betrayed the value the founders placed on high character as essential to preserving public trust in the office of the presidency. The importance of character, and the risk that a president whose character would prove lacking might strive to become a tyrant, contributed to the decision to provide impeachment as the ultimate safety valve for the Republic. By the time Congress impeached Trump the issue of his character had long been settled, so no one (including his allies) appeared to hold him to a measurable moral standard.

It is worth noting that two of the three impeachment stories that follow took place before the Supreme Court held that freedom of expression extends to factual falsehoods in its 2012 *United States* v. *Alvarez* decision. However, *Alvarez* does not seem to have altered the impeachment landscape.

1. Richard M. Nixon, A.K.A. "Tricky Dick"

The House of Representatives never voted to impeach President Richard M. Nixon. He resigned under pressure from leaders of his own Republican Party who warned him that the impeachment process then under way and ultimate conviction by the Senate were imminent. Yet the bill of impeachment adopted by a House committee, but never brought to a vote, remains a critical building block in my analysis.

Nixon was a gutter fighter and a master of deception, until he wasn't. Early in his career he earned the nickname "Tricky Dick" as he red-baited with the best of them and smeared opponents. He engaged in numerous acts of deception while successfully seeking the presidency in 1968 and then while serving as president. Many of his misleading statements and false denials concerned the conduct and expansion of undeclared wars in Southeast Asia.

None of those deceptions led to the threat of inevitable impeachment that convinced Nixon to resign abruptly in 1974. Instead, the events that led to Nixon's demise began with acts that were incontrovertibly illegal, such as burglary. Resort to crimes, according to historians, "became not only an available option but central to the President's conception of the office of chief executive of the United States."[4] The list of criminal offenses committed at Nixon's direction would require too long a detour to review here.

The 1972 break-in to plant wiretaps at the offices of the Democratic National Committee in Washington, D.C.'s Watergate Hotel during Nixon's campaign for reelection proved his undoing. Nixon and his team embarked on a massive cover-up designed to impede discovery of their role in the Watergate break-in; they presciently feared an investigation would reveal their many other crimes.

Nixon's malfeasance was firmly established through congressional hearings, evidence turned up by Special Prosecutor Leon Jaworski after his predecessor had been fired in the aptly named Saturday Night Massacre, and a unanimous Supreme Court decision ordering the White House to turn over subpoenaed evidence. After publication of the "smoking gun" Oval Office tapes with their inexplicable 18½-minute gap, and more, the Judiciary Committee of the House of Representatives voted on a bipartisan basis to send a bill of impeachment to the House floor for a vote. The bill of particulars included both abuse of power and obstruction of justice, virtually the same charges Donald Trump would confront in his first impeachment a half century later.

The very first article of impeachment against Nixon charged him with lying to the American people: "making false or misleading public statements for the purpose of deceiving the people" about the origins and cover-up of the Watergate break-in. Nixon had lied when he assured the public that no one at the White House or in a responsible position in his reelection campaign had been involved. This string of events gave rise to the truism that the cover-up entraps more politicians than the underlying offense. Nixon's lies to the public implicated other enumerated charges in the articles of impeachment such as obstruction of justice and failure to perform his "constitutional duty to 'take care that the laws be faithfully executed.'"

The Nixon bill of impeachment would have provided a firmer precedent about lying to the public as an impeachable offense if it had reached the House floor and been adopted, and if the Senate had then convicted him. It is undeniable that Nixon did the country a service by resigning, even if he deprived us of a solid precedent. Congress never repudiated lying to the public as a ground for removing a president.

In the aftermath of Nixon's resignation, as Congress considered various proposals for reform, a panel of eminent scholars convened by the American Enterprise Institute warned that any "comprehensive" attempt to "regulate [political] 'smears,' however desirable it may seem," would "necessarily raise First Amendment questions."[5] However, the panel—chaired by Yale law professor Ralph K. Winter Jr., who later became a federal appellate judge— stopped short of parsing what those First Amendment pitfalls might be.

The proposals the panel referenced were relatively limited. They aimed at smears and deceptions during political campaigns, speech that Chapter 4 explained cannot be regulated without violating the First Amendment. As far as I am aware, Congress has never had occasion to consider whether the Constitution permits penalties for public deception by current officeholders while not under oath or outside campaign activities.

No public body appears to have revisited the relationship between lies during and about elections, lies by presidents, and the Speech Clause until the beginning of 2021, when it arose in the context of Trump's second impeachment trial (discussed later in this chapter). Even then, the issue evaded comprehensive analysis and resolution.

2. William J. Clinton, Louche Liar

The articles of impeachment the House of Representatives adopted in 1998 against President William J. Clinton—perjury and obstruction of justice— both targeted dishonesty. Although he was charged with lying under oath and not with lying to the public, Clinton's false public denials intensified his image as a liar. The *New York Times* subsequently reported that when then- senator Joseph Biden learned that President Clinton had lied about his inti- mate relationship with a White House intern, he wanted to "punch him right square in the nose."[6]

Clinton's alleged sexual advances and admitted extramarital affairs (most famously with White House intern Monica Lewinsky) and his effort to conceal them led him to prevaricate at press conferences and under oath. When the Supreme Court rejected Clinton's contention that he could not be forced to defend against a civil lawsuit while in office, Clinton was ordered to submit to a sworn deposition in a civil suit brought by Paula Jones. Jones alleged that, while governor of Arkansas, Clinton had made unwelcome sexual advances in a hotel room. At the secret request of Independent Counsel Kenneth Starr, Jones's lawyers used the deposition to probe Clinton about his relationship with Monica Lewinsky. Clinton did not answer truthfully.

After the Lewinsky story broke, Clinton dishonestly assured the public, "I did not have sexual relations with that woman." Clinton claimed that what he said was "legally accurate" because whatever else he and Monica Lewinsky did, they never had sexual intercourse. It does not matter whether that declaration was a bald-faced lie, an intentional distortion, or a prevarication. Americans learned that they had been played. Clinton failed to offer the transparency his political opponents and much of the public sought.[7]

Although the narrow issue in Clinton's impeachment centered on his lies under oath, Lindsey Graham, at that time a member of the House of Representatives and one of the House managers presenting the case against Clinton to the Senate, addressed the president's lies more broadly. Sketching the narrative of what Clinton did, Graham told the Senate: "He got caught off guard [about his relationship with Lewinsky] and he started telling a bunch of lies that maybe I would have lied about. Maybe you would have lied about." But presidents are held to a higher standard, Graham explained: "Impeachment is about cleansing the office. Impeachment is about restoring honor and integrity to the office." It is for when presidents "get out of bounds." Graham warned that the impact of acquitting Clinton would be "devastating." The case had forced "parents and teachers to sit down and explain what lying's all about."[8]

Clinton's legal problems persisted after the Senate, voting on partisan lines, acquitted him. Federal judge Susan Webber Wright, who was presiding over the Paula Jones case, held Clinton in contempt for having given "intentionally false" deposition testimony. Judge Wright chastised Clinton for his "false, misleading and evasive answers" and referred him to the Arkansas Supreme Court for potential disbarment proceedings. Clinton settled the disbarment matter by admitting he "knowingly gave evasive and misleading answers" in his sworn deposition, accepting a five-year suspension of his Arkansas license to practice law, and paying a $25,000 fine.[9]

Both Nixon and Clinton lied to the public. Those public lies did not violate any statute. But public trust eroded when they broadcast factual falsehoods about matters on which their political detractors and the public were fixated. Fifty years ago and twenty years ago, respectively, those lies seemed like a big deal. The founders would have agreed that the lies were out of bounds and violated the public trust.

Congressional Oversight of Lies

Treating the president as a public employee as I suggested in the last chapter raises logistical concerns. It is easy to outline the mechanics of workplace discipline for public employees whose position in a chain of command is clear, but who supervises a lying president?

The lies Trump told and the harm they directly caused would have qualified as high crimes and misdemeanors in the founders' eyes. Application of public employee speech doctrine to mendacious presidents complements the founders' vision. Invoking it would fortify the power of impeachment for lying to the public. It should eviscerate the claim that the First Amendment immunizes a president's dangerous or even seditious rhetoric from being treated as a high crime and misdemeanor.

The concept that "the president works for us" does more than fortify the force of impeachment; it offers an alternate route to presidential accountability. Translated into a narrowly tailored congressional resolution that forbids certain forms of presidents' harmful speech, as detailed later in this chapter, it would add to the tools of congressional oversight that stop short of impeachment.

If readers accept my argument that public employee doctrine can constitutionally be applied to presidents, especially if limited to carefully defined lies, two questions still require resolution: Who has the power to discipline the president? How would they do it?

The short answer to both questions is Congress, through a sliding scale of actions starting with oversight hearings and culminating in impeachment with all that can follow, and the overhanging threat of criminal indictment where warranted.

One may worry that my proposal would chill presidential expression. That is exactly the point. Presidents have no license to tell lies that endanger the Republic or our very lives. Application of a narrowly construed public employee speech doctrine to a clearly delineated set of presidential lies—set out in the previous chapter—should put to rest any potential First Amendment claims a mendacious president might offer.

The Constitution assigns to Congress the grave responsibility of overseeing the president. In *Nixon v. Fitzgerald*, anticipating in 1982 an objection that immunity from civil suit would render the president "above the law," the Supreme Court pointed to constitutional provisions directed at constraining presidential "misconduct." The majority hit hard: "There remains the constitutional remedy of impeachment." Presidents, the majority mused, are presumed to be concerned about how the public views them and about their "historical stature." In case those personal restraints prove insufficient, however, "vigilant oversight by Congress also may serve to deter Presidential abuses, as well as to make credible the threat of impeachment."[10]

Those prophylactic and disciplinary measures had much greater vitality in 1982 than they appear to possess today, but their availability as a matter of law remains intact.

Congressional Power to Interpret High Crimes and Misdemeanors

Since, as *Fitzgerald* advises, the impeachment power gives teeth to congressional oversight, we begin by asking whether Congress has the power to interpret what constitutes a high crime and misdemeanor, and to include lying—narrowly construed—within that definition. If Congress lacked that power, any steps it took to constrain presidential lies would be mere posturing. But my analysis indicates that Congress must have the ultimate power to interpret the grounds for impeachment.

We start by revisiting in greater depth what the phrase "high crimes and misdemeanors" meant to the founders. The language was drawn from English common law, where it had been applied often enough to have a comprehensible meaning.

The remedy is broadly intended to reach far beyond the criminal code to encompass "crimes against the state." Congressional reports have concluded that impeachable offenses embrace wrongs that "undermine the integrity of office and even the Constitution itself" as well as "misconduct that damages the state and the operations of government institutions."[11]

Impeachment was the remedy, Alexander Hamilton explained in Federalist 65, for "abuse or violation of some public trust," that is, "injuries done immediately to the society itself." The injuries highly placed officials can inflict on society, the social fabric, and constitutional governance would not normally appear in a criminal code. The range of actions that can betray public trust is so extensive that it would be difficult to reduce them to writing.

The framers intentionally left the precise scope of the grounds for impeachment vague; the offense must be serious, like treason or bribery, but the text does not spell out the exact parameters. Hamilton explained the reasoning. The nature of the impeachment remedy counsels against framing "strict rules" that would govern "the delineation of the offense" so that Congress would retain the flexibility to respond to a variety of situations that could warrant impeachment.[12]

The Impeachment Clause is not unique in this respect. In the 1819 case of *McCulloch* v. *Maryland*, the Supreme Court explained that a constitution designed to "contain an accurate detail" resembling that of a legal code "could scarcely be embraced by the human mind." Therefore, its "nature . . . require[s] that only its great outlines should be marked."[13] The legislature and the courts must continually fill in the details.

Constitutional doctrine indicates that Congress is empowered to determine the meaning of high crimes and misdemeanors. Express interpretation of what is included in high crimes and misdemeanors would not require revisions to the constitutional language; it would merely be a gloss (or authoritative comment) on existing terminology, one that Congress is uniquely situated to provide.

Because Congress has never attempted to codify any of the grounds for impeachment beyond the constitutional language, relying instead on precedents and a case-by-case formulation, there has never been an occasion to determine whether Congress has the power to clarify the grounds for impeachment as a general matter. That Congress has never acted to define high crimes and misdemeanors outside a unique impeachment proceeding does not mean it lacks the power to do so.

Context and constitutional structure support the conclusion that Congress is fully empowered to flesh out the meaning of high crimes and misdemeanors. By assigning to Congress the task of overseeing the president and, if necessary, impeaching him, the Constitution left the definition of impeachable behavior to Congress. Two lines of reasoning lead from this proposition to the conclusion that Congress is authorized to define impeachable offenses, if it chooses, through legislation, so long as it preserves the flexibility the framers envisioned.

The first line of reasoning was set out by Neal Katyal, Georgetown law professor, MSNBC legal commentator, and former acting solicitor general of the United States, who has argued, "Congress has interpretive supremacy over other branches" when it comes to impeachment. Katyal points to several grounds for assuming that Congress rather than the judiciary controls constitutional interpretation of the grounds for impeachment. One is that Congress is subject to political accountability at the next election. Voters will have a chance to approve or disapprove congressional actions after the impeachment proceeding and trial. Federal judges, in contrast, have lifetime appointments.[14]

Equally important, the federal courts are not likely to address the constitutionality of a ground for impeachment. The Supreme Court has already ruled that Congress may choose the procedures it will use for impeachments, so long as it satisfies the conditions for presidential impeachment and trial: the senators must be sworn as jurors, the chief justice must preside, and two-thirds of those present must vote guilty to sustain a conviction.[15]

The grounds for impeachment are a prototype of a "political question," a category of issues the court declines to answer, and even deems "nonjusticiable" or not suitable for judicial resolution. This leaves Congress as the only branch of government with the capacity to interpret the constitutional provisions governing impeachments.

A second line of reasoning rests on the Constitution's structure. Article I, Section 8 enumerates eighteen legislative powers of Congress, leading some to conclude that Congress lacks authority to act on any other matters. The eighteenth paragraph—known as the Necessary and Proper Clause—authorizes Congress to "make all Laws" necessary and proper for executing its enumerated powers, "and all other Powers vested by this Constitution in the Government of the United States, or in any Department or Officer thereof." Broad as that clause sounds, it is not a general grant of any and all powers.

However, other sections of and amendments to the Constitution grant Congress additional legislative powers to effectuate constitutional goals. Eleven clauses in the body of the Constitution and another fourteen in the amendments expressly create such powers.[16]

Article II governs the executive branch. Section 1 of Article II provides that Congress may determine the date and time when the delegates to the Electoral College shall cast their votes. Based on that provision, Congress codified detailed procedures for perfecting the electors' decision through laws enacted in 1887 and amended in 1948.[17]

It is unclear which of those clauses gives Congress the authority to legislate detailed certification procedures, but no one to my knowledge has asserted that Congress lacks the power to enact statutes governing the final steps in determining the result of presidential elections. By analogy, congressional authority to impeach and remove a president from office presumably vests Congress with the power to interpret the constitutional language governing the grounds for those momentous actions, and if it chooses, to do so through legislation.

Escalating Oversight and Remedies

Impeachment is a drastic measure. Absent emergencies (like an attempted coup or a president who welcomes foreign troops to invade), impeachment should never be the first step when it becomes necessary for Congress to rein in a president. Other forms of supervision are available to Congress before it considers impeachment. They include notice; oversight hearings; and censure. Only then should Congress reach impeachment, conviction, and removal followed by disqualification; where appropriate, criminal prosecution may follow.

Notice

Initially, I envision Congress articulating its normative expectations about the level of honesty it expects from presidents. Notice that lies may be impeachable seems especially imperative where Congress seeks to establish or restore norms that recent presidents have gutted.

Congress could alert future presidents that moving forward it does not intend to tolerate rampant presidential lies (as I have defined them or in some other narrow formulation). People generally have the right to clear warning about what acts violate the criminal code, and the need for notice is especially critical when speech rights might be implicated. While the presidential lies discussed in this book would not normally amount to criminal speech, and behavior does not need to violate the criminal code to be impeachable, congressional discipline portends ominous consequences for a president.

Any notice of congressional intent to hold presidents accountable for material falsehoods should define the scope of the targeted lies. It should warn the president that Congress has concluded that a pattern of material verifiable factual falsehoods falls within the sweep of the "high crimes and misdemeanors" for which impeachment is warranted.

If Congress labels presidential lies as high crimes and misdemeanors it should expressly reserve its continuing discretion to interpret the phrase on a case-by-case basis as it has done historically. Doing so would foreclose a future president's argument that Congress had limited the broad scope of impeachable offenses.

Several mechanisms exist for communicating notice that presidential lies are subject to congressional discipline. First, Congress could pass a law, which would have to be signed by the president or adopted by a two-thirds majority of each house overriding a presidential veto. In a Rawlsian world of blindfolded decision making, a government that did not anticipate the need to tame presidential mendacity any time soon might pass such a statute. In the world we occupy today, both political parties would likely be reluctant to create a weapon that could be used against a future president of their party.

Second, Congress could adopt resolutions, which would not require either a presidential signature or agreement of both houses. If the two houses agree on language, they could adopt a concurrent resolution. But either house could adopt a resolution on its own. This approach has serious limitations because resolutions merely express the sense of the current Congress. Since resolutions lack legal authority, they must be accompanied by the threat of concrete actions to have any impact beyond political performance.

Giving notice to future presidents serves two functions. First, it warns a prudent president to exercise caution when tempted to misrepresent material facts. Second, notice setting out distinct boundaries could also simplify the congressional task if and when Congress confronts a future mendacious president. Congress would not need to make an individualized determination in the context of a particular impeachment proceeding about whether presidential lies fall within the scope of high crimes and misdemeanors. It could move directly to the question of whether the utterances at issue meet the existing definition of presidential lies, limiting a potentially contentious preliminary debate. As we saw in the case of Judge Michael Gableman (described in Chapter 4), however, reaching agreement on whether particular words fit within a legal definition of lies may not be a straightforward proposition.

None of the ways of providing notice would effect permanent change. A future Congress could rescind the warning about presidential lies regardless of whether it was communicated by a statute or by resolutions. But that would be a dangerous path because recision would appear to expressly welcome presidential mendacity.

And yet recision is not the only way a mendacious president's allies can signal that lies can escape accountability. Partisan enabling of particular presidential lies, such as President Trump's insistence that he won the 2020 election by a landslide, establishes the point. After all, as described in Chapter 1, most Republican members of Congress denied or refused to admit that Joe Biden had won the presidency even after the Electoral College voted on December 14, 2020. And a substantial number of Republicans in Congress voted not to certify certain election results on January 6, 2021. Days after the Senate acquitted Trump in his second impeachment trial, nearly a month after Biden had been sworn in, forty-five of the fifty Republican senators still refused to commit themselves when CBS asked, "Do you agree with President Trump that he—and not Joe Biden—won the November election?"[18] The question remained relevant because even as CBS asked it Trump was on cable news repeating that he had won a large victory.

If Congress were to rescind previous instructions regarding its expectations of truthfulness, it would communicate that presidents have free rein to lie to us. At that point, our democracy would already be in such decline that all bets would be off.

Hearings

Oversight hearings normally constitute the first step for all potential congressional remedies, absent a need for emergency intervention. Hearings focused on the president's veracity about matters of public significance could be scheduled on a regular basis or only in response to specific speech incidents that trigger alarms.

History indicates that a mendacious president is likely to try to impede congressional inquiries, especially those that might lead to impeachment. Imperiled presidents have denied Congress documents, asserted executive privilege even where it does not apply, discouraged witnesses from testifying or ordered them not to appear, and battled congressional requests for information in court. Obstruction may succeed in blocking a committee's ability to understand or prove executive misbehavior. It can even drag an inquiry out until the president's term has ended. For hearings on presidential lies or misdeeds to be effective, Congress must be prepared to invoke all of its powers—including subpoenas and contempt citations—against a recalcitrant executive branch.

Lying presidents may also try to avoid responsibility by outsourcing lies to political appointees such as press secretaries or cabinet members. The president may be held accountable through the legal construct of "agency" when executive branch political appointees deceive the public, including the press, or when those officials lie under oath to protect him. (Individual officials who perjure themselves under oath would, of course, remain subject to prosecution.)

Agency imposes responsibility on an individual (known as the "principal," here, the president) who authorizes another (designated the "agent," for example the press secretary or a cabinet officer) to act on his behalf. Agents represent the president when they speak. If the president fails to correct high officers when they tell verifiable falsehoods or does not correct the public record, the agent's acts and words can also be attributed to the president. Agency theory is legally enforceable, unlike "The buck stops here" sign on President Harry S. Truman's desk.

Following hearings that reveal a pattern of material verifiable factual falsehoods, Congress could warn the president to cease and desist. A letter from a congressional committee or from congressional leaders, or a resolution—any direct means of communication would serve the purpose. Each of those methods lacks enforceable legal significance, but any of them would afford the president an opportunity to correct the record by retracting his own lies or lies offered to the public on his behalf.

Censure

In an arguably stronger step, Congress—or either chamber—might adopt a censure resolution. Like other resolutions, censure lacks legal significance unless directed at a member of Congress. Censure expresses the "sense of" the body. A resolution could urge the president to correct the record or stop repeating the material falsehoods but would have no formal impact if the president ignored the message.[19]

These concerns explain why House Speaker Nancy Pelosi rejected the notion that some moderates, including Republicans, floated of censuring

President Trump after the Senate acquitted him for the second time in February 2021. She derided censure as a "slap on the wrist" for someone who used "stationery for the wrong purpose."[20]

Alternatively, a resolution could call for the president to resign, but there is little reason for a president to comply. A president's scorn for such a request could further weaken the congressional hand.

The same holds true for any congressional request that the vice president invoke the Twenty-Fifth Amendment, which provides for the temporary removal of a mentally or physically incompetent president. It initially requires the vice president and a majority of the cabinet to find the president unable to perform his or her duties. If they are not prepared to begin that process, it seems unlikely that a prod from Congress would inspire them to act.

Last Stop: Impeachment

If the approaches discussed above fail, as they are likely to do, Congress should be prepared to impeach a lying executive and to remove that president from office. That step should not be taken cavalierly. However, the body politic should not have to wait until damage is inflicted while a lying president injures society itself, as President Trump did during the COVID-19 pandemic and in assaulting the Constitution while striving to overturn the 2020 election results.

Treating the president as a public employee for the limited purpose of containing presidential lies would allow Congress to initiate impeachment even if the materially harmful words are not accompanied by nefarious conduct, allowing it to head off grievous harm. Imagine if the House of Representatives had impeached and the Senate convicted President Trump when he unleashed his stream of lies about election fraud. Congress could have acted during the build up to the election, when Trump prepared his voters to deny his potential loss, after the election when he continued to falsely claim a landslide victory, or after he refused to accept the Electoral College vote on December 14. Had Congress responded forcefully to those lies— collectively, a frontal attack on the Constitution—it might well have prevented the insurrection of January 6.

Presidents require full First Amendment protection for their policies and politics, no matter how much Congress disagrees with those choices. Nor can they be impeached for what the founders called "maladministration," which amounts to not doing a good job. That is why Congress was powerless to respond to administrative failures in the face of COVID-19.

But a focus on dangerous presidential lies might have provided a pathway to congressional action when Trump undermined the country's COVID-19 response. Congress could have started by informing Trump that his falsehoods about the virus put him at risk of censure and more. Other presidents might have responded by changing their tone, while Trump might well have ignored the warning—forcing Congress, if it were willing to act, to take additional measures. Such a warning could have sharpened the issue, increased pressure on the chief executive, and either constrained his lies or hastened the impeachment process.

Explosive Truths

Lies are not the only words that might trigger impeachment: explosive truths might also meet the high crimes and misdemeanors standard. For example, on July 30, 2020, one of Trump's tweets began with the familiar lies: "2020 will be the most INACCURATE & FRAUDULENT Election in history. It will be a great embarrassment to the USA." But then he broke into a startling revelation of his real motivation, which was not to prevent fraud but to "Delay the Election" he feared he would lose. That outburst was followed by false insinuations that people would not be able to "securely and safely vote" on November 3 and concluded "???" to indicate he was testing the waters.[21]

In response, Northwestern University School of Law professor Steven Calabresi, co-founder of the very conservative Federalist Society, immediately urged Congress to impeach Trump. It was quite a turnaround. Calabresi had defended Trump during the first impeachment proceedings earlier that year. Now Calabresi labeled Trump's tweet with a term he had previously condemned: "fascistic." Calabresi did not specify the grounds for impeachment and did not consider whether the Speech Clause protected Trump's remarkably revealing words.[22]

A president who speculates about postponing an election, without having taken any concrete steps toward that goal, or who seeks to overturn election results after losing decisively (for example, by truthfully tweeting his wish to #OVERTURN), creates grounds for impeachment. The words are truthful in the sense that they convey the speaker's actual aspiration. Unless the statements meet the legal grounds for treason, the offense is limited to speech—to be sure, speech that attacks constitutional governance. But the words violate the president's constitutional obligation to "take Care that the Laws be faithfully executed." Conceptualizing presidents as public employees helps explain why the First Amendment does not protect their seditious tweets though it protects others who might post #OVERTURN.

Like lies, explosive truths are more dangerous coming from presidents. A president could and should be impeached for announcing, "My goal is a frontal attack on the Constitution" or "I am going to give the keys to the Oval Office to a foreign dictator." Neither statement could be barred under a criminal statute without violating the Speech Clause. But both pronouncements would betray the president's oath to "preserve, protect, and defend the Constitution of the United States."

Calabresi is right that Congress should move vigorously to remove a self-proclaimed would-be autocrat from office. Treating a president as an employee would remove a president's potential freedom of expression defense against impeachment whether the words that threaten the nation's survival are false or truthful.

The Trials of Donald J. Trump

We return in closing to the man who by all accounts was the most prodigious, impulsive, and egregious liar in the history of the presidency, Donald J. Trump. He was not directly charged with lying to the public in either of his impeachments, though he had done so repeatedly. However, Trump's lies about the 2020 election ran through the bill of particulars the second time he was impeached and tried.

The first time it impeached President Trump in December 2019, the House of Representatives cited only two of the many potential grounds created since the beginning of his term: abuse of power and obstruction of Congress. The charges stemmed from Trump's now-infamous telephone call with the Ukrainian president. During that call Trump attempted to extort the Ukrainian president by threatening to withhold appropriated funds Ukraine needed to defend itself against Russia and dangling the prospect of an Oval Office visit conditioned on Ukraine initiating a public investigation of Joe Biden's son Hunter. Trump hoped to use the initiation of that investigation to derail Biden's prospects of gaining the Democratic nomination and winning the 2020 election.

The 2019 Articles of impeachment charged that Trump had covered up the substance of that phone call and then sought to impede the resulting congressional investigation. Trump's lies to the public about what he called a "perfect" telephone call resembled the lies Nixon and Clinton told, but they were not included in the express charges against him.

After he escaped conviction and removal from office on February 5, 2020, Trump ramped up the pace and audacity of his deceptions. Why wouldn't he? All of the Republican senators except for Mitt Romney had voted to acquit after refusing to call a single witness, signaling to the president that they had his back no matter what he did.

That free pass doubtless encouraged the lies that followed, including the two streams of destructive deception chronicled earlier in this book: the falsehoods about COVID-19 analyzed in Chapter 5 and the Big Lie about the 2020 election discussed in Chapter 1. The latter led to the deadly insurrection at the Capitol on January 6, 2021.

The House of Representatives impeached Trump for the second time one week after the seditious assault on the Capitol. In the words of Mitch McConnell, the outgoing Republican Senate majority leader, who would later vote to acquit Trump: "The mob was fed lies. They were provoked by the president."[23] The bipartisan vote in the House captured the urgency of the moment—the fear that a president who had incited a violent invasion of the Capitol in a vain effort to hold onto power might do even more unimaginable things in the two remaining weeks of his term.

The January 2021 Article of Impeachment adopted by the House was limited to one count: the "high crime and misdemeanor of Incitement of Insurrection." The particulars put issues of free speech and deception front and center for the first time in any presidential impeachment proceeding.

Every reader knows the outcome. Despite overwhelming evidence of Trump's culpability, affirmed beyond doubt by McConnell's renewed excoriation of Trump's words and actions immediately after he voted not guilty along with all but seven members of his party, the former president was acquitted. This is not the place for a retrospective of Trump's second impeachment trial.

The discussion here centers on the First Amendment issues the trial brought into focus. Both sides floated or implied theories and questions about the place of the First Amendment in impeachment proceedings generally, about a president's speech rights, and about the power of presidential lies that remain unresolved.

In an impeachment trial, no judge rules on what the law is. No one instructs the jurors about the law that binds their decision. And there is no penalty for jurors who reject the rules they themselves have established, as many Republican senators did when they continued to insist that they lacked power to try an impeached president after his term ended, despite a Senate vote rejecting that proposition.

Let us again start with a preliminary question: Do First Amendment rights have any role in impeachment proceedings?

Trump's defense rested in large part on the assertion that Trump's speech "fell well within the norms of political speech that is protected by the First Amendment." His lawyers read the First Amendment's command, "Congress shall make no law," to apply to all congressional actions.[24]

More than 140 constitutional law scholars refuted that claim in an open letter (which I signed) explaining that the First Amendment does not apply to impeachment proceedings. An impeachment proceeding is not a criminal trial; illegal conduct is not required for impeachment. The tirade by Trump that led the House to impeach did not need to meet the criminal definition of the incitement he was charged with, because impeachment did not depend on Trump committing an unlawful act. It rested on violation of his oath of office.[25]

If the Supreme Court had considered the merits of this dispute and concluded that the guarantees of the First Amendment have no place in impeachments, then I might have abandoned the last two chapters of this book. There would be no need to rely on the public employee speech doctrine to avoid violating a president's expressive rights. But no court has ruled on this important question.

Incitement

If we rely on the common understanding of the term "incite," Trump's rhetoric indisputably incited the riotous mob on January 6. Representative Liz Cheney, a leader of the House Republicans, summed up what had happened: "The President of the United States summoned this mob, assembled the mob, and lit the flame of this attack. Everything that followed was his doing."[26]

However, if a president can claim First Amendment protection in the face of congressional discipline, the initial question would be whether

Trump's January 6 speech to the mob met the *legal* definition of incitement. If the First Amendment applies, then incitement that falls short of the Supreme Court's definition applicable to criminal prosecution might provide a defense.

Readers may recall that the Speech Clause does not protect incitement. Similar to defamation, freedom of expression requires legal conditions designed to make incitement difficult to prove in order to protect zealous advocacy. The Supreme Court set out the test for criminal incitement in *Brandenburg* v. *Ohio*, decided in 1969. The court proclaimed that freedom of speech protects even "advocacy of the use of force" or of illegal acts, "except where such advocacy is directed to inciting or producing imminent lawless action and is likely to incite or produce such action."[27]

At a criminal trial the prosecution would have to establish beyond a reasonable doubt that Trump satisfied every element of the *Brandenburg* test. In contrast, individual senators choose their own standard of proof for convicting a president. In criminal trials, the federal rules of evidence and procedure apply, barring hearsay, and requiring the state to call witnesses who would be subject to cross-examination. Some evidence would probably be excluded. None of those limitations apply in a Senate proceeding.

In applying the *Brandenburg* test, reasonable jurors in a federal court would be tasked with determining whether Trump "directed" or "produce[d]" the violence on January 6 and whether violence was "likely" to occur in response to his speech. Imminence should be more than satisfied by Trump's exhortation to walk right now to the Capitol. This—"let's go right now"—is the example law professors use to teach the concept of imminence.

If the Senate or individual senators opted to use the criminal standard established in *Brandenburg*, the distinctions in the rules of evidence and the standard of proof between Senate and criminal trials make it at least plausible that two-thirds of the senators could vote to convict a president on the same facts that could lead a criminal jury to acquit. A reasonable jury in a criminal trial could conclude that Trump's inflammatory rhetoric fell short of directing violence or that the state had failed to prove beyond a reasonable doubt that violence had been the likely response to his speech. But a jury might also reasonably answer those questions the other way, and convict on these facts.

And so, even if the Senate had applied *Brandenburg*, it could have held Trump accountable, especially after placing his words in context as the test requires. Context also informs a common sense understanding of incitement. It allows us to take into account what the speaker said and did before the allegedly incendiary speech, and how the speaker responded to the violence that followed.

The Senate never specified whether it was using the *Brandenburg* standard in considering whether Trump incited violence, but it could have relied instead on colloquial and moral understandings of what it means to incite. That approach presumably would also take context into account.

The second Article of Impeachment filed against Trump in 2021 provided context. It relied heavily on lies that preceded his inflammatory January 6 speech and on the lies he continued to spread after the insurrection began. At the Ellipse just as Congress gathered in joint session to certify the election results on January 6, Trump exhorted the crowd with a mixture of lies (the election was "stolen") and explosive truths that conveyed his true intentions ("fight like hell" to a crowd that had declared itself on social media to be ready for violence). The Article of Impeachment charged that Trump "reiterated false claims that 'we won this election, and we won it by a landslide.'" "Reiterated" refers to what Trump said in the months leading up to that: he "repeatedly issued false statements asserting that the Presidential election results were the product of widespread fraud and should not be accepted by the American people or certified by State or Federal officials."[28]

Like Nixon, Trump lied to the American people. Going beyond Nixon, Trump's lies inspired an armed mob to attack our government.

The Public Employee Approach

The incitement case against former President Trump illustrates the benefits of applying public employee speech doctrine. Doing so would circumvent any potential First Amendment defense. Congress could focus exclusively on whether the expression it seeks to discipline meets its definition of presidential lies. And Congress could act before the falsehoods caused predictable grievous harm.

Treating the president as a public employee would also allow Congress to hold presidents to account for a class of falsehoods that would not satisfy the prevailing legal definition of a lie. If Trump actually believed he won the election by a landslide, that would be irrelevant if he persisted in the claim after being presented with the verifiable facts to the contrary. So too, Congress could constrain unwarranted assertions about "magical" authority, whether they sprang from demagogic intent, lack of information, or literal delusion, so long as the assertion materially affected the body politic. It would not matter whether the president knew no magical powers existed or had intended to deceive others. The fact of the verifiably false utterance and the specter of harm to the body politic it raises would suffice for disciplinary purposes if the president is treated as a public employee.

Both instances, "Trump won" and magical powers, exemplify the kinds of expression that would be protected for any other citizen, but that should be subject to regulation precisely because the words are the president's. Average people and even celebrities presumably present less of a hazard than presidents do when they call COVID-19 a hoax or baselessly accuse others of election fraud.

Other Avenues of Accountability

Invocation of congressional remedies neither rules out nor substitutes for other ways of holding mendacious presidents to account beyond voting them out of office. Public repudiation, civil lawsuits, and criminal prosecution remain.

All of the remedies available to Congress are fully compatible with criminal prosecution in a parallel or a subsequent proceeding. Article I, Section 3 cl.7 of the Constitution specifically instructs that the impeached party who has been removed from office following conviction by the Senate "shall nevertheless be liable and subject to Indictment, Trial, Judgment and Punishment, according to Law." Of course, criminal indictment would only be appropriate where the presidential lie violated a valid criminal statute or facilitated other crimes.

Notwithstanding current policy, the Constitution implies through silence that it is permissible to prosecute a sitting president. Indictment is currently unavailable because Department of Justice opinions issued in 1973 and 2000 established an internal policy against indicting presidents while they remain in office. The department's opinions are memoranda that can be discarded at any time. They erect a formidable barrier for federal prosecutors who are not allowed to indict a president as long as the opinions remain in place and the president remains in office. However, state and local prosecutors, free of supervision by the federal Department of Justice, may indict a sitting president without violating any law or constitutional provision.

There is no shortage of constitutional mechanisms for disciplining a mendacious president. But they have largely been abandoned by members of Congress who put political calculations above their oaths of office and, in the case of the most recent Senate trials, above their oaths as jurors.

Contemporary Impediments to Accountability

In the wake of the Senate's second acquittal of former president Trump, impeachment may not appear a credible weapon against a demagogic executive. For all practical purposes, it seems that the majority of Republican senators have vitiated the impeachment, conviction, and removal mechanism, throwing our government of co-equal branches completely out of balance. Disabling the fail-safe remedy the founders bequeathed to us puts the country at grave risk.

Although Trump provided many of the examples I used in exploring the constitutional status of lies, the proliferation of factual falsehoods and misinformation in public discourse began long before he assumed office. It has not abated since his term ended. Indeed, in the months after President Biden's inauguration, Republican leaders in the states and in Congress continued to promote Trump's unsubstantiated claims that the 2020 election had been stolen.

In Arizona, the Republican-dominated state senate authorized a novice private contractor who had proclaimed the 2020 election illegitimate to conduct an unofficial recount of the ballots in Maricopa, the state's largest county. Maricopa had already undergone two official audits which found no major irregularities. The contractors took possession of the original ballots, jeopardizing any future accountability. As the purported audit dragged on, Maricopa's county recorder, an elected Republican, broke ranks, tweeting: "We can't indulge these insane lies any longer. As a party. As a state. As a country."[29]

Taken in by those lies and other verifiable falsehoods, months into the Biden presidency nearly one-third of *all* voters told Reuters/Ipsos pollsters that they agreed the "2020 election was stolen from Donald Trump." Commitment to baseless conspiracy theories remained even stronger among Republicans, 60 percent of whom believed that the 2020 election results were illegitimate.[30]

Relying on disinformation and the public skepticism about electoral legitimacy that they themselves had stoked, Republicans pursued flagrant efforts to suppress voting. Starting with Georgia, at least thirty-three state legislatures with Republican majorities adopted or proposed new laws that would restrict access to voting. Some of those statutes would also allow state officials to overturn local vote tallies. Proponents of those flagrant restrictions asserted it was important to reassure the voters who believed the 2020 election had been marred by irregularities even if no fraud had actually occurred. In essence, they proclaimed that verifiable facts are less relevant than unfounded beliefs.

Several clarifying incidents converged on May 12, 2021. First, members of the House Republican caucus purged Liz Cheney of her leadership position because she persisted in calling out the pervasive lies. Her specific sins: reiterating Trump's role in provoking the January 6 insurrection and her truthful statement that "Our election was not stolen."

The day before she was stripped of her leadership position, Cheney addressed a nearly empty House chamber condemning Trump's "aggressive effort to convince Americans that the election was stolen from him." That lie, she said, "risks inciting further violence" and "undermine[s] our democratic process." Cheney urged her colleagues to "speak the truth." Their oath of office, she said, obligates members of Congress to "act to prevent the unraveling of our democracy." She added ominously, "Remaining silent, and ignoring the lie, emboldens the liar."[31]

The next day, within hours after the Republican caucus purged Cheney, House minority leader Kevin McCarthy (who had orchestrated her removal) made what seemed like a momentous statement after his first meeting with President Biden, telling the press, "I don't think anybody is questioning the legitimacy of the presidential election."[32]

McCarthy's denial of the partisan attack on the legitimacy of Biden's election was disingenuous at best. Not only had House Republicans just fired Cheney for refusing to go along with the Big Lie, many Republican office-holders at every level amplified the stolen election mythology that former president Trump still promulgated almost daily. The "anybody" McCarthy falsely asserted did not question the election's legitimacy also included 124 retired generals and admirals who had just released an unprecedented public letter promoting the false narrative that in 2020 the United States was deprived of "fair and honest elections that accurately reflect the 'will of the people.'"[33]

That is not all that happened on May 12. At a House committee hearing on the January 6 insurrection, Republicans continued their months-long effort to distort the facts. Representative Andrew Clyde of Georgia, for one, who was captured in a photo on January 6 trying to barricade the House chamber as rioters strove to break through the doors, denied anything untoward had happened that day; he even compared the armed mob to "a normal tourist visit."[34] Other Republican committee members joined him in downplaying what happened on January 6. Several also denied that the invaders were Trump supporters, ignoring the photos showing the rioters in Trump paraphernalia, their public statements, and numerous disclosures that the hundreds of people arrested included Trump zealots, Proud Boys, and Oathkeepers.

The most potent obstacle to constraining a mendacious president is not found in the Speech Clause but rather in the toxic forces that define our contemporary political condition. At present, those forces are concentrated on the right of the political spectrum; false equivalence would deny that empirical reality. Strident partisanship, a Republican party more enamored of power than of facts or policy goals, and a breakdown of collaboration in Congress, seem to render my proposals for reining in presidential mendacity virtually unattainable in the immediate future.

That said, to presume that the nation will not be able to restore norms of collaborative governance would be a premature and self-defeating surrender. Under current circumstances, my proposals respecting presidential lies would ideally be discussed in the context of a comprehensive strategy for shoring up our democracy.

Conclusion

Truth is essential to democracy, while lies subvert it like ivy vines that cause mortar to crumble. Informed political debate collapses absent shared verifiable facts and perceptions of reality. Truth, as historian Sophia Rosenfeld has argued, is more than a practical requirement; it is at least as "foundational" as "liberty and equality and happiness."[35]

However, no simple solution for pervasive public falsehoods exists in the United States. Legal efforts to proscribe lies, it should be clear by this point, cannot generally overcome First Amendment strictures that prevent the government from labelling and punishing most falsehoods—including bald-faced lies, no matter who gives voice to them. First Amendment doctrine makes clear that government efforts to regulate falsehoods would inevitably undermine the robust debate at the heart of the Speech Clause.

Even if the Constitution permitted official efforts to constrain lies, who would identify the harmful falsehoods subject to penalty? If anyone still doubts that the government cannot be trusted to arbitrate between truth and falsehood, the events of May 12, 2021—including a party pillorying its truth-teller while office holders and retired military leaders promoted blatant falsehoods, disregarding truths that did not suit them—should lay that doubt to rest. No one should assume that an arbiter of truth would share their worldview and values or be an honest broker. Government officials who promulgate falsehoods can be expected to label lies as truth and vice versa when they have the power to do so.

Those constitutional constraints do not create an affirmative right to lie. Some falsehoods are encompassed in long-standing exceptions to the protection of the Speech Clause. Other lies, the Supreme Court has intimated, might be subject to penalty because they harm others or unjustly advantage the liar.

But many questions remain unanswered. The Supreme Court has not elaborated on what harms or advantages might be sufficiently compelling to support penalties for additional types of falsehoods. Nor, as I have explained, has the court advised judges what standard of review applies to lies, which would determine whether the government needs to show a compelling interest for suppressing falsehood or merely a significant one. Small wonder confusion persists about whether there is a right to lie.

Despite those complexities, which prohibit a simple yes or no answer to the question posed in the title of this book, I have demonstrated that presidents have no more right to lie than anyone else. If there is a will to stop a dangerously mendacious president, constitutional structure and doctrine provide a way. This conviction leaves me cautiously optimistic about the long term.

Among other things, the burden of combatting factual falsehoods does not rest on public officials alone. The First Amendment assigns roles to the press and to individuals.

The press is hardly a monolith. It comprises traditional journalists who champion the ethos of truth as well as purveyors of propaganda, such as Fox News, that many people accept as legitimate news sources. The task of combating rampant disinformation and conspiracy theories spread by Fox, One

America, and similar outlets and online by the likes of QAnon raises a host of First Amendment concerns that would require additional volumes to address.

The rhetorical construct of a free market in ideas may never have accurately captured how ideas prevail and may well have overestimated the power of more and better speech. That dilemma seems even more intractable today as online speech—free from any guardrails and capable of metastasizing rapidly—dominates public debate.

And yet, the most responsible press outlets still play a critical role in seeking out and presenting reliable facts that can help people distinguish what information is trustworthy. Individuals, to whom courts considering defamation claims impute a responsibility to assess everything they read and hear, bear the same burden in the public sphere: to apply reason and common sense.

Partisans from each of the leading epistemic tribes surely believe themselves to be the only patriots, but in truth they do not have equal claims. One tribe alone—core Republicans—bears primary responsibility for promulgating, promoting, and swearing by the factual falsehoods and unsubstantiated claims that led to the January 6 insurrection aimed at the Constitution itself. In the absence of recantation by those who promoted insurrection and subsequently denied its import, the burden of safeguarding democracy will not be evenly distributed.

This brings us to the ordinary citizens who believe that truth matters and that lies matter. Democrats, Independents, disenchanted and former Republicans, they must voice "more and better" speech at least as strongly as those who choose to deny fact-based reality insist on their beliefs.

Beyond speaking out, active citizens who value truth should give substance to their convictions by insisting that all citizens have access to voting and by voting in every election cycle. Voters may hold lying elected officials accountable. They can also demand that Congress and other institutions impose consequences on mendacious officials who work for us.

If that happens, it could be possible to curb ubiquitous falsehoods in the public square without abandoning our constitutional commitment to free speech. The unthinkable alternative would be to abandon the fight to protect and perfect our democracy.

NOTES

Citations are provided for direct quotations from former President Trump delivered on specific dates, but not for comments he repeated that are easily found online.

A brief guide to legal references: The abbreviations to the F. Supp. Series refer to the volumes containing District Court (federal trial level) opinions; F., F.2d, and F.3d contain federal appellate court opinions; and U.S. refers to decisions of the Supreme Court, except for the most recent, which appear as S. Ct. State court opinions are published in a variety of reporters; the state is indicated in parentheses. Other citations indicate that the opinion or court filing has not been published.

Chapter 1

1. Tim Malloy and Doug Schwartz, "59% Say Trump Should Not Be Allowed to Hold Office in Future, Quinnipiac University National Poll Finds; 2 out of 3 Republicans Do Not Think Biden's Victory Is Legitimate," Quinnipiac University Poll, Jan. 18, 2021, https://poll.qu .edu/images/polling/us/us01182021_usyn921.pdf.

2. Bernd Kaussler, Lars J. Kristiansen, and Jeffrey Delbert, *Rhetoric and Governance Under Trump: Proclamations from the Bullshit Pulpit* (Lanham, MD: Lexington Books, 2020), 163, 289.

3. Glenn Kessler et al., "A Term of Untruths: The Longer Trump Was President, the More Frequently He Made False or Misleading Claims," *Washington Post*, Jan. 23, 2021.

4. Russ Buettner, Susanne Craig, and Mike McIntire, "The President's Taxes: Long-Concealed Records Show Trump's Years of Chronic Losses and Years of Tax Avoidance," *N.Y. Times*, Sept. 27, 2020.

5. Dan Alexander, "Donald Trump Has at Least $1 Billion in Debt, More Than Twice the Amount He Suggested," *Forbes*, Oct. 16, 2020; William D. Cohan, "Trump's Tax Mess Aside, Can He Pay Off His $1 Billion in Debt?," *Vanity Fair*, Oct. 1, 2020.

6. Neha Prakash, "Donald Trump Freaks Out on Twitter After Obama Wins Election," Mashable, Nov. 6, 2012, https://mashable.com/2012/11/06/trump-reacts-to-election/.

7. Charles M. Blow, "Trump's Campaign of Chaos," opinion, *N.Y. Times*, Aug. 23, 2020; Mattathias Schwartz, "Obama Had a Secret Plan in Case Trump Rejected 2016 Election Results," Intelligencer, Oct. 10, 2018.

8. Richard L. Hasen, "Trump's Relentless Attacks on Mail-In Ballots Are Part of a Larger Strategy," opinion, *N.Y. Times*, Aug. 19, 2020.

9. Hasen, "Trump's Relentless Attacks"; Trip Gabriel, "The Election Day Nightmare Democrats Dread," *N.Y. Times*, Sept. 3, 2020, A1, A18; Donald J. Trump (@realDonaldTrump), Twitter, June 22, 2020, 7:16 A.M; Donald J. Trump (@realDonaldTrump), Twitter, June 22, 2020, 9:45 A.M.

10. Donald J. Trump (@realDonaldTrump), Twitter, Sept. 17, 2020, 7:36 A.M.

11. Andrew Romano, "New Yahoo News/YouGov Poll: Only 22% of Americans Think the 2020 Presidential Election Will Be 'Free and Fair,'" Yahoo News, Sept. 18, 2020; Aila Slisco, "Just One Third of Americans Think the Election Will Be Free and Fair: Poll." *Newsweek*, Oct. 14, 2020.

12. "Election Fraud Database," Heritage Foundation, accessed Feb. 10, 2021, https://www.heritage.org/voterfraud; "Debunking the Voter Fraud Myth," Brennan Center for Justice, Jan. 31, 2017, https://www.brennancenter.org/sites/default/files/analysis/Briefing_Memo_Debunking_Voter_Fraud_Myth.pdf.

13. "A Democratic Stress Test—The 2020 Election and Its Aftermath," Bright Line Watch, accessed Feb. 10, 2021, http://brightlinewatch.org/a-democratic-stress-test-the-2020-election-and-its-aftermathbright-line-watch-november-2020-survey/.

14. Motion for Leave to File Bill of Complaint, Texas v. Pennsylvania, No. 220155, Original (U.S. Dec. 7, 2020), https://www.supremecourt.gov/DocketPDF/22/220155/162953/20201207234611533_TX-v-State-Motion-2020-12-07%20FINAL.pdf; Motion for Leave to File Brief Amicus Curiae, Texas v. Pennsylvania, No. 220155, Original (U.S. Dec. 10, 2020), https://www.supremecourt.gov/DocketPDF/22/220155/163550/20201211132250339_Texas%20v.%20Pennsylvania%20Amicus%20Brief%20of%20126%20Representatives%20—%20corrected.pdf; Texas v. Pennsylvania, No. 220155, ORIG. (U.S. Dec. 11, 2020), https://www.supremecourt.gov/orders/courtorders/121120zr_p860.pdf.

15. H.R. Res. 24, 117th Cong. (2021); Complaint and Demand for Jury Trial at 67, US Dominion, Inc. v. Giuliani, No. 1:21-cv-00213 (D.D.C. Jan. 25, 2021).

16. Donald J. Trump (@realDonaldTrump), Twitter, Jan. 6, 2021, 6:01 P.M.; Donald J. Trump (@realDonaldTrump), Twitter, Jan. 6, 2021, 2:24 P.M.

17. Emily Badger, "Most Republicans Say They Doubt the Election. How Many Really Mean It?," *N.Y. Times*, Dec. 1, 2020, A18.

18. Paul Kane and Scott Clement, "Just 27 Congressional Republicans Acknowledge Biden's Win, *Washington Post* Survey Finds," *Washington Post*, Dec. 5, 2020.

19. Richard Fausset, "'It Has to Stop': Georgia Election Official Lashes Trump," *N.Y. Times*, updated Jan. 7, 2021.

20. Elizabeth Dwoskin and Craig Timberg, "Misinformation Dropped Dramatically the Week after Twitter Banned Trump and Some Allies," *Washington Post*, Jan. 16, 2021.

21. Joel T. Nadler and Tiffany Edwards, "Big Lie Technique," in *Encyclopedia of Deception*, ed. Timothy R. Levine (Thousand Oaks, CA: Sage Publications, 2014), 78–79, https://www.dx.doi.org/10.4135/9781483306902.n30. The immediate origins of the proposition are traceable to Adolf Hitler's *Mein Kampf*, though the first use of the purported quote has never been identified.

22. Ruth Ben-Ghiat, *Strongmen: Mussolini to the Present* (New York: W. W. Norton, 2020), 9.

23. Steven Levitsky and Daniel Ziblatt, *How Democracies Die* (New York: Crown, 2018), 198–199, 23–24.

24. Timothy Snyder, *On Tyranny: Twenty Lessons from the Twentieth Century* (New York: Tim Duggan Books, 2017), 66–68.

25. Sissela Bok, *Lying: Moral Choice in Public and Private Life*, 2nd ed. (New York: Vintage Books, 1999), xvii, 13, 16.

Chapter 2

1. Brief for Respondent at 1, *United States* v. *Alvarez*, 567 U.S. 709 (2012) (No. 11-210); *United States* v. *Alvarez*, 567 U.S. 709, 714 (2012).

2. *United States* v. *Alvarez*, 617 F.3d 1198, 1201 (9th Cir. 2010).

3. 18 U.S.C. § 704(b) (2012).

4. *United States* v. *Alvarez*, 617 F.3d at 1217.

5. Sissela Bok, *Lying: Moral Choice in Public and Private Life*, 2nd ed. (New York: Vintage Books, 1999), 43.

6. Quoted in Bok, *Lying*, 40.

7. Harry G. Frankfurt, *On Bullshit* (Princeton, NJ: Princeton University Press, 2005), 5–7 (quoting and discussing Max Black, *The Prevalence of Humbug and Other Essays* [Ithaca, NY: Cornell University Press, 1983]).

8. *United States* v. *Alvarez*, 567 U.S. at 733 (Breyer, J., concurring).

9. *United States* v. *Alvarez*, 638 F.3d 666, 673–675 (9th Cir. 2011) (Kozinski, C.J., concurring in the denial of rehearing en banc).

10. Jim McElhatton, "Exposer in Stolen Valor Case Fired: 10-Year Marine Heard Boasts as Corporate Host," *Washington Times*, Mar. 6, 2012.

11. *Alvarez*, 638 F.3d at 673 (Kozinski, C.J., concurring).

12. Dan Ariely, *The (Honest) Truth About Dishonesty: How We Lie to Everyone—Especially Ourselves* (New York: HarperCollins, 2012), 165.

13. 10 U.S.C. § 7271 (Army); 10 U.S.C. § 8291 (Navy and Marine Corps); 10 U.S.C. § 9271 (Air Force); 14 U.S.C. § 2732 (Coast Guard).

14. *Alvarez*, 567 U.S. at 741–42 (Alito, J., dissenting); H.R. Rep. No. 113-84, at 2 (2013).

15. Stolen Valor Act of 2013, Pub. L. No. 113-12, 127 Stat. 448.

Chapter 3

1. Gertz v. Welch, 418 U.S. 323, 344 n.9 (1974).

2. N.Y. Times Co. v. Sullivan, 376 U.S. 254, 268 (1964).

3. *Sullivan*, 376 U.S. at 272 (quoting NAACP v. Button, 371 U.S. 415, 433 (1963)), 270 (quoting United States v. Associated Press, 52 F.Supp. 362, 372 (S.D.N.Y. 1943) (Hand, J.)).

4. *Sullivan*, 376 U.S. at 271–273.

5. Adam Serwer, "Birtherism of a Nation," *Atlantic*, May 13, 2020.

6. "WorldNetDaily," Southern Poverty Law Center, accessed Feb. 28, 2021, https://www .splcenter.org/fighting-hate/extremist-files/group/worldnetdaily.

7. Farah v. Esquire Mag., 736 F.3d 528, 530 (D.C. Cir. 2013) (the facts and the discussion of the law that follow are all drawn from this opinion).

8. Liberty Lobby v. Anderson, 746 F.2d 1563, 1568 n.6 (D.C. Cir. 1984).

9. United States v. Alvarez, 567 U.S. 709, 719 (2012).

10. Milkovich v. Lorain J. Co., 497 U.S. 1, 20 (1990); Weyrich v. New Republic, 235 F.3d 617, 620, 623 (D.C. Cir. 2001) (Edwards, C.J.) (citing Moldea v. N.Y. Times Co., 15 F.3d 1137, 1142–43 (D.C. Cir. 1994)).

11. *Alvarez*, 567 U.S. at 720.

12. Spence v. Flynt, 816 P.2d 771, 774 (Wyo. 1991).

13. Hustler Mag., Inc. v. Falwell, 485 U.S. 46 (1988).

14. Finkel v. Dauber, 906 N.Y.S.2d 697, 702 (N.Y. Sup. Ct. 2010).

15. *Milkovich*, 497 U.S. at 16–17 (discussing Greenbelt Coop. Publ'g Ass'n, Inc. v. Bresler, 398 U.S. 6, 13 (1970)).

16. New Times, Inc. v. Isaacks, 146 S.W.3d 144, 149, 161, 157, 154, 158 (Tex. 2004) (citations omitted).

17. *Isaacks*, 146 S.W.3d at 149.

18. *Farah*, 736 F.3d at 540 (quoting *Milkovich*, 497 U.S. at 21).

19. Memorandum of Law in Support of Defendants' Motion to Dismiss, US Dominion, Inc. v. Sidney Powell, No. 1:21-cv-00040-CJN (D.D.C. Mar. 22, 2021), 27–28, 32, 37.

20. Peter Baker and Maggie Astor, "Trump Pushes a Conspiracy Theory That Falsely Accuses a TV Host of Murder," *N.Y. Times*, May 26, 2020.

21. Baker and Astor, "Trump Pushes a Conspiracy Theory."

22. Baker and Astor, "Trump Pushes a Conspiracy Theory."

23. Complaint, Donald J. Trump for President, Inc. v. CNN Broad., Inc., No. 1:20-cv-01045 (N.D. Ga. Mar. 6, 2020) (dismissed Nov. 12, 2020); Complaint, Donald J. Trump for President, Inc. v. N.Y. Times Co., No. 152099/2020 (N.Y. Sup. Ct. Feb. 26, 2020) (dismissed Mar. 9, 2021); Complaint for Damages, Donald J. Trump for President, Inc. v. WP Co., No. 1:20-cv-00626 (D.D.C. Mar. 3, 2020) (motion to dismiss pending).

24. Orders on Petitions for Review, Infowars, LLC v. Fontaine, No. 19-1029 (Tex. Jan. 22, 2021); Orders on Petitions for Review, Jones v. Pozner, No. 19-1102 (Tex. Jan. 22, 2021); Orders on Petitions for Review, Jones v. Heslin, No. 20-0347 (Tex. Jan. 22, 2021).

25. E.g., Complaint and Demand for Jury Trial at 2, US Dominion, Inc. v. Giuliani, No. 1:21-cv-00213 11CJN-CJN (D.D.C. Jan. 25, 2021).

26. The Lincoln Project (@ProjectLincoln), "Your False and Defamatory Statements about the Lincoln Project (with Accompanying Notice to Preserve All Relevant Documents, If Any)," Twitter, Jan. 30, 2021, 3:46 P.M., https://twitter.com/ProjectLincoln/status/1355618315570393090.

Chapter 4

1. Lauren Carroll and Linda Qiu, "Looking Back at Lie of the Year," PolitiFact, Dec. 13, 2016; Charles M. Blow, "In Defense of the Truth," opinion, *N.Y. Times*, Sept. 4, 2017; Angie Drobnic Holan, "2017 Lie of the Year: Russian Election Interference Is a 'Made-Up-Story,'" PolitiFact, Dec. 12, 2017.

2. Terri Cullen, "Second-Quarter GDP Plunged by Worst-Ever 31.7% as Economy Went into Lockdown," CNBC, Aug. 27, 2020; OECD, "Unprecedented Falls in GDP in Most G20 Countries in Second Quarter of 2020," Sept. 14, 2020, https://www.oecd.org/economy/g20-gdp-growth-second-quarter-2020-oecd.htm; Jeff Cox, "Payrolls Increase by Nearly 1.4 Million as the Unemployment Rate Tumbles," CNBC, updated Sept. 30, 2020.

3. Daniel Dale, "We Had an Avalanche of Lying from President Trump," interview by Wolf Blitzer, CNN, Sept. 29, 2020.

4. Steph Bazzle, "Fact-Checkers Counted Every Lie Trump Told—Now They Say There Are Too Many to Count," *The Hill*, Oct. 30, 2020.

5. Ashley Parker, "Trump and Allies Ratchet Up Disinformation Efforts in Late Stage of Campaign," *Washington Post*, Sept. 6, 2020.

6. Parker, "Trump and Allies"; Roudabeh Kishi and Sam Jones, "Demonstrations and Political Violence in America: New Data for Summer 2020," Armed Conflict Location & Event Data Project, Sept. 30, 2020, https://acleddata.com/2020/09/03/demonstrations-political-violence-in-america-new-data-for-summer-2020/.

7. Harry G. Frankfurt, *On Bullshit* (Princeton, NJ: Princeton University Press, 2005), 5–7.

8. Monitor Patriot Co. v. Roy, 401 U.S. 265, 274–275 (1971).

9. Fla. Stat. Ann. § 104.271; Miss. Code Ann. § 23-15-875.

10. Richard L. Hasen, "A Constitutional Right to Lie in Campaigns and Elections?," *Montana Law Review* 74, no. 1 (Winter 2013): 63; Rossen v. Tarkanian, 453 P.3d 1220 (Nev. 2019).

11. "Read the Full Transcript from the First Presidential Debate between Joe Biden and Donald Trump," *USA Today*, updated Oct. 4, 2020; Mike Reese (@SheriffReese), Twitter, Sept. 29, 2020, 10:07 p.m., https://twitter.com/SheriffReese/status/1311125507757416449. On October 12, Reese tweeted he was honored to "ACTUALLY endorse @Joe Biden & @Kamala Harris."

12. Fla. Stat. Ann. § 104.271.

13. Jennifer Steinhauer, "Confronting Ghosts of 2000 in South Carolina," *N.Y. Times*, Oct. 19, 2020.

14. George Orwell, "Appendix: The Principles of Newspeak," in *1984* (New York: Signet Classics, 1977), 305–10, 305.

15. George Orwell, "Appendix," 305.

16. United States v. Alvarez, 567 U.S. 709, 716, 723 (2012) (Kennedy, J., plurality opinion) (quoting Ashcroft v. American Civil Liberties Union, 535 U.S. 564, 573 (2002)); *Alvarez*, 567 U.S. at 752 (Alito, J., dissenting).

17. N.Y. Times v. Sullivan, 376 U.S. 254, 271 (1964).

18. *Sullivan*, 376 U.S. at 271.

19. Ariz. Free Enter. Club's Freedom Club PAC v. Bennett, 564 U.S. 721, 734 (2011) (quoting Eu v. San Francisco Cnty. Democratic Cent. Comm., 489 U.S. 214, 223 (1989)).

20. Harte-Hanks Communications, Inc. v. Connaughton, 491 U.S. 657, 687 (1989) (quoting Jonathan Elliot, ed., *The Debates in the Several State Conventions on the Adoption of the Federal Constitution*, 2nd ed. ([Philadelphia: J. B. Lippincott, 1861], 4:575).

21. Burson v. Freeman, 504 U.S. 191, 199 (1992).

22. Commonwealth v. Lucas, 34 N.E.3d 1242, 1253 (Mass. 2015).

23. Anderson v. Celebrezze, 460 U.S. 780, 782 (1983).

24. *Lucas*, 34 N.E.3d at 1253.

25. *Alvarez*, 567 U.S. at 725 (Kennedy, J., plurality opinion); Brown v. Ent. Merchants Ass'n, 564 U.S. 786, 799 (2011).

26. Rickert v. Pub. Disclosure Comm'n, 168 P.3d 826, 831 (Wash. 2007); ACLU of Nev. v. Heller, 378 F.3d 979, 996–97 (9th Cir. 2004).

27. Meghan Keneally, "Arizona Congressional Candidate Changes His Name to Cesar Chavez in Order to Appeal to Hispanic Voters," *Daily Mail*, June 3, 2014; Jaime Fuller, "This Arizona Candidate Changed His Name. His Opponent Wasn't Happy About It," *Washington Post*, June 12, 2014.

28. Utah Code Ann. § 20A-11-1103; Colo. Rev. Stat. § 1-13-109.

29. Pub. Disclosure Comm'n v. 119 Vote No! Comm., 957 P.2d 691, 700 (Wash. 1998).

30. *Pub. Disclosure Comm'n*, 957 P.2d at 695.

31. Republican Party of Minn. v. White, 536 U.S. 765 (2002) (Scalia, J.); Williams-Yulee v. Fla. Bar, 575 U.S. 433, 446 (2015).

32. Gableman for Supreme Court, "Prosecutor," last accessed Feb. 28, 2021, video, :31, https://youtu.be/KUiK4ruhVUk.

33. Dee J. Hall, "Gableman Wins Supreme Court Race," *Chippewa Herald*, Apr. 7, 2008, https://chippewa.com/news/gableman-wins-supreme-court-race/article_572804b4-4352-53c4-a15b-627dc9608ce5.html.

34. In re Jud. Disciplinary Proc. Against Gableman, 784 N.W.2d 605, 612 (Wis. 2010) (Abrahamson, C.J.) (quoting Judicial Conduct Panel's Findings of Fact, Conclusions of Law and Recommendations at 10 (No. 2008AP2458-J) (Deininger, J., concurring)), https://www .wicourts.gov/news/archives/2009/docs/gableman.pdf.

35. Judicial Conduct Panel's Findings of Fact, *Gableman*, 784 N.W.2d 605 (No. 2008AP 2458-J) at 19, 17 n.1, 15 n.10.

36. *Gableman*, 784 N.W.2d at 617 (Abrahamson, C.J.); In re Judicial Disciplinary Proceedings Against Gableman, 784 N.W.2d 631, 646–47 (Wis. 2010) (Prosser, J.).

37. *Gableman*, 784 N.W.2d at 613, 615 (Abrahamson, C.J.).

38. *Gableman*, 784 N.W.2d at 641–44 (Prosser, J.).

39. Jessica VanEgeren, "Capitol Report: Judicial Commission Files Complaint: Justice Prosser Asserts His Innocence," *Cap Times*, updated May 22, 2012, https://madison.com/ct /news/local/govt-and-politics/capitol-report/capitol-report-judicial-commission-files -complaint-justice-prosser-asserts-his-innocence/article_fe38b81c-6fb0-11e1-84dd -001871e3ce6c.html; Wis. Jud. Comm'n v. Prosser, 827 N.W.2d 605 (Wis. 2013).

40. *Gableman*, 784 N.W.2d at 616 n.34 (Abrahamson, C.J.) (quoting Judicial Conduct Panel's Findings of Fact, *Gableman*, 784 N.W.2d 605 (No. 2008AP2458-J)).

41. Reed v. Gallagher, 204 Cal. Rptr. 3d 178, 193 (Cal. Ct. App. 2016)(citations omitted); In re Callaghan, 796 S.E.2d 604, 627 (W. Va. 2017)(citations omitted).

42. *In re Callaghan*, 796 S.E.2d at 627 (quoting Turner v. KTRK Television, Inc., 38 S.W.3d 103, 115 (Tex. 2000)).

43. *Gableman*, 784 N.W.2d at 614 (Abrahamson, C.J.).

Chapter 5

1. Scottie Andrew, "The US Has 4% of the World's Population but 25% of Its Coronavirus Cases," CNN, updated June 30, 2020; Claire Lampen, Hannah Gold, and Amanda Arnold, "Everything to Know about the Coronavirus in the United States," The Cut, updated Dec. 13, 2020, https://www.thecut.com/2020/12/which-states-have-coronavirus-and-how-do-you-minimize -risk.html.

2. Bob Woodward, *Rage* (New York: Simon & Schuster, 2020), 325.

3. Maggie Haberman, "Trade Adviser Warned White House in January of Risks of a Pandemic," *N.Y. Times*, updated Apr. 17, 2020.

4. Woodward, *Rage*, 294.

5. Jamie Gangel, Jeremy Herb, and Elizabeth Stuart, "'Play It Down': Trump Admits to Concealing the True Threat of Coronavirus in New Woodward Book," CNN, Sept. 9, 2020; Joe Biden, "Flashback by Joe Biden: Trump Is Worst Possible Leader to Deal with Coronavirus Outbreak," opinion, *USA Today*, Jan. 27, 2020.

6. Woodward, *Rage*, xix, 260, 294.

7. Woodward, *Rage*, 285.

8. Woodward, *Rage*, 296.

9. Sheryl Gay Stolberg and Noah Weiland, "President Perpetuates Falsehoods, Study Finds," *N.Y. Times*, Oct. 1, 2020, A9; Sarah Evanega et al., "Coronavirus Misinformation: Quantifying Sources and Themes in the COVID-19 'Infodemic,'" Cornell Alliance for Science, Department of Global Development, Cornell University, 2020, https://allianceforscience .cornell.edu/wp-content/uploads/2020/10/Evanega-et-al-Coronavirus-misinformation -submitted_07_23_20-1.pdf.

10. Matt Stevens, Isabella Grullón Paz, and Jennifer Medina, "Kristin Urquiza, Whose Father Died of Covid, Denounces Trump at D.N.C.," *N.Y. Times*, Aug. 17, 2020.

11. Michael D. Shear, "'We've Had No Negative Effect and We've Had 35–40,000 People,'" *N.Y. Times*, Sept. 30, 2020, A18.

12. Shear, "'We've Had No Negative Effect,'" A18; B. Douglas Bernheim et al., "The Effects of Large Group Meetings on the Spread of COVID-19: The Case of Trump Rallies," Institute for Economic Policy Research (SIEPR), Stanford University, 2020.

13. Mark Walker and Jack Healey, "Bitter Fallout of Bikers' Rally," *N.Y. Times*, Nov. 7, 2020, A1, A5.

14. Quoted in Thomas B. Edsall, "'I Fear That We Are Witnessing the End of American Democracy,'" opinion, *N.Y. Times*, Aug. 26, 2020.

15. Caitlin O'Kane, "Trump Said Coronavirus 'Affects Virtually Nobody,' as U.S. Surpasses 200,000 Deaths," CBS News, updated Sept. 22, 2020.

16. Savannah Behrmann, "'You're Not Someone's Crazy Uncle': Guthrie Challenges Trump on Conspiracy Theory Retweets," *USA Today*, Oct. 15, 2020.

17. Robert Farley, "Trump Has Not Been 'Clear' in Support of Masks," FactCheck.org, Sept. 25, 2020, https://www.factcheck.org/2020/09/trump-has-not-been-clear-in-support-of -masks/.

18. Marshall Allen and Meg Marco, "How Your Brain Tricks You into Taking Risks during the Pandemic," ProPublica, Nov. 2, 2020.

19. Lara Bull-Otterson et al., "Hydroxychloroquine and Chloroquine Prescribing Patterns by Provider Specialty Following Initial Reports of Potential Benefit for COVID-19 Treatment—United States, January–June 2020," *Morbidity and Mortality Weekly Report* 69, no. 35 (Sept. 4, 2020): 1210, http://dx.doi.org/10.15585/mmwr.mm6935a4.

20. "Remarks by President Trump, Vice President Pence, and Members of the Coronavirus Task Force in Press Briefing" (remarks, Washington, DC, Mar. 19, 2020), White House, https://trumpwhitehouse.archives.gov/briefings-statements/remarks-president-trump-vice -president-pence-members-coronavirus-task-force-press-briefing-6/; What do you have to lose?: "Remarks by President Trump, Vice President Pence, and Members of the Coronavirus Task Force in Press Briefing" (remarks, Washington, DC, Apr. 4, 2020), White House, https:// trumpwhitehouse.archives.gov/briefings-statements/remarks-president-trump-vice -president-pence-members-coronavirus-task-force-press-briefing-19/; "NIH Halts Clinical Trial of Hydroxychloroquine," National Institutes of Health, June 20, 2020, https://www.nih .gov/news-events/news-releases/nih-halts-clinical-trial-hydroxychloroquine; Libby Cathey, "Timeline: Tracking Trump Alongside Scientific Developments on Hydroxychloroquine," ABC News, Aug. 8, 2020; Andrew Joseph, "WHO Drops Hydroxychloroquine from Covid-19 Clinical Trial," STAT, June 17, 2020, https://www.statnews.com/2020/06/17/who-drops -hydroxychloroquine-covid-19-clinical-trial/.

21. Trudy Rubin, "Trump's Promotion of 'Demon Sperm' Doctor Bodes Ill for Any Second Term," opinion, *Philadelphia Inquirer*, July 30, 2020; Moustafa Bayoumi, "Why Is Donald Trump Jr Amplifying a Quack Who Believes in 'Demon Sperm'?" opinion, *Guardian* (US edition), July 29, 2020; Travis M. Andrews and Danielle Paquette, "Trump Retweeted a Video with False Covid-19 Claims. One Doctor in It Has Said Demons Cause Illnesses," *Washington Post*, July 29, 2020.

22. Joseph Guzman, "In a Newly Released Tape, Trump Says COVID-19 Is 'a Killer' That 'Rips You Apart,'" *The Hill*, Sept. 15, 2020.

23. Jessica Guynn, "Facebook, Twitter Remove Trump Coronavirus Posts of Fox Interview About Kids Being 'Almost Immune,'" *USA Today*, updated Aug. 6, 2020.

24. Donald J. Trump, "Remarks by President Trump in Press Briefing" (remarks, Washington, DC, Aug. 10, 2020), https://trumpwhitehouse.archives.gov/briefings-statements/remarks-president-trump-press-briefing-august-10-2020/.

25. Alex Woodward, "Trump Repeats False Claim Children Are 'Immune' to Coronavirus Despite 97,000 Infections Among Young People Reported in July," *Independent* (UK), Aug. 11, 2020; *Children and COVID-19: State-Level Data Report* (American Academy of Pediatrics, Oct. 2020).

26. Noah Higgins-Dunn, "U.S. Reports Second-Highest Daily Number of Covid Cases on Election Day as Scientists Warn of a Dangerous Winter," CNBC, updated Nov. 6, 2020; Lauren Leatherby, "United States Records Its Worst Week Yet for Virus Cases," *N.Y. Times*, Oct. 30, 2020.

27. Tom Nichols, *The Death of Expertise: The Campaign against Established Knowledge and Why It Matters* (New York: Oxford University Press, 2017), 17–20, 211.

28. Isaac Chotiner, "The Contrarian Coronavirus Theory That Informed the Trump Administration," *New Yorker*, Mar. 30, 2020; Jonathan Chait, "Richard Epstein Can't Stop Being Wrong about the Coronavirus," Intelligencer, Apr. 21, 2020.

29. Colleen Flaherty, "Not Shrugging Off Criticism," Inside Higher Ed, Sept. 23, 2020; Ashley Collman, "The Rise and Fall of White House COVID-19 Advisor Dr. Scott Atlas, a Lockdown Skeptic Who Had Trump's Ear and Fought with Experts like Fauci," Business Insider, Dec. 1, 2020; Michael Gerson, "Here Are the Trump Administration's Four Most Profound Failures in the Pandemic," opinion, *Washington Post*, Oct. 27, 2020.

30. Anita Chabria et al., "21 on Cruise Ship Test Positive; Passengers Show Anger, Worry over Coronavirus," *Los Angeles Times*, Mar. 7, 2020, B1.

31. Morgan Chalfant, "Trump: 'With Smaller Testing We Would Show Fewer Cases,'" *The Hill*, June 23, 2020.

32. Donald J. Trump (@realDonaldTrump), Twitter, Nov. 2, 2020, 1:35 P.M.; Glenn Kessler (@GlennKesslerWP), Twitter, Nov. 2, 2020, 1:39 P.M., https://twitter.com/glennkesslerwp/status/1323333954888437760.

33. Charles Piller, "Federal System for Tracking Hospital Beds and COVID-19 Patients Provides Questionable Data," *Science*, Nov. 29, 2020.

34. Jennifer Bendery, "Leaked Reports Show White House Knew of COVID-19 Spike as Trump Downplayed Crisis," HuffPost, Oct. 20, 2020.

35. Christopher J. L. Murray, "Why Is Virus Data Kept Secret?," opinion, *N.Y. Times*, Oct. 24, 2020, A23.

36. Domenico Montanaro, "Poll: Americans Don't Trust What They're Hearing from Trump on Coronavirus," NPR, Mar. 17, 2020; "Coronavirus Polling," Axios/Ipsos, Wave 29, Oct. 23–26, 2020, https://www.ipsos.com/sites/default/files/ct/news/documents/2020-12/topline-axios-wave-33.pdf; Alexander Burns and Jonathan Martin, "Voters Prefer Biden over Trump on Almost All Major Issues," *N.Y. Times*, Oct. 20, 2020.

37. Burns and Martin, "Voters Prefer Biden over Trump"; Katie Thomas, David Gelles, and Carl Zimmer, "Vaccine Is over 90% Effective, Pfizer's Early Data Says," *N.Y. Times*, Nov. 10, 2020, A1, A5; Frances Stead Sellers, "Now That There's a Coronavirus Vaccine, How Do You Persuade People to Take It?," *Washington Post*, Dec. 11, 2020.

38. Nigel Chiwaya and Corky Siemaszko, "Covid-19 Cases, Deaths Rising Rapidly Ahead of Election Day," NBC News, Nov. 2, 2020.

39. Andrew E. Budson, "The Hidden Long-Term Cognitive Effects of COVID-19," *Harvard Health Blog*, Oct. 8, 2020; Stephen J. Elledge, "2.5 Million Person-Years of Life Have Been Lost Due to COVID-19 in the United States" (unpublished manuscript, Oct. 27, 2020), https://doi.org/10.1101/2020.10.18.20214783.

40. Sen Pei, Sasikiran Kandula, and Jeffrey Shaman, "Differential Effects of Intervention Timing on COVID-19 Spread in the United States," *Science Advances* 6, no. 49 (Dec. 2020), https://doi.org/10.1126/sciadv.abd6370; "New IHME COVID-19 Model Projects Nearly 180,000 US Deaths," IHME, University of Washington, June 24, 2020, http://www.healthdata.org/news-release/new-ihme-covid-19-model-projects-nearly-180000-us-deaths.

41. Anthony Komaroff, "The Tragedy of Post-COVID 'Long Haulers,'" *Harvard Health Blog*, Oct. 15, 2020; Budson, "Hidden Long-Term Cognitive Effects."

42. Komaroff, "Tragedy of Post-COVID"; Budson, "Hidden Long-Term Cognitive Effects"; Ed Yong, "Long-Haulers Are Redefining COVID-19," *Atlantic*, Aug. 19, 2020.

43. Elledge, "2.5 Million Person-Years of Life Have Been Lost."

44. Mark É. Czeisler et al., "Mental Health, Substance Use, and Suicidal Ideation During the COVID-19 Pandemic—United States, June 24–30, 2020," *Morbidity and Mortality Weekly Report* 69, no. 32 (Aug. 14, 2020): 1049; Catherine K. Ettman et al., "Prevalence of Depression Symptoms in US Adults Before and During the COVID-19 Pandemic," *JAMA Network Open* 3, no. 9 (Sept. 2, 2020); Maxime Taquet et al., "Bidirectional Associations Between COVID-19 and Psychiatric Disorder: Retrospective Cohort Studies of 62354 COVID-19 Cases in the USA," *Lancet Psychiatry* 8, no. 2 (Feb. 2021)..

45. "Out of Work in America," *N.Y. Times*, Oct. 23, 2020.

46. "USA Inc's Ponderous Recovery," *Economist*, Nov. 7, 2020; Matthew Haag, "One-Third of New York's Small Businesses May Be Gone Forever," *N.Y. Times*, Aug. 3, 2020.

47. Jason DeParle, "Why Hunger Can Grow Even When Poverty Doesn't," *N.Y. Times*, July 28, 2020 (using the federal figure that takes location into account); Zachary Parolin et al., "Monthly Poverty Rates in the United States During the COVID-19 Pandemic" (working paper, Center on Poverty and Social Policy, Columbia University, Oct, 15, 2020), 9–10; Jeehoon Han, Bruce D. Meyer, and James X. Sullivan, "Income and Poverty in the COVID-19 Pandemic" (NBER Working Paper no. 27729, Aug. 2020), https://www.nber.org/papers/w27729.

48. Emily Benfer et al., *The COVID-19 Eviction Crisis: An Estimated 20–40 Million People in America Are at Risk* (National Low Income Housing Coalition, Aug. 7, 2020).

49. NPR, Robert Wood Johnson Foundation, and Harvard T. H. Chan School of Public Health, *The Impact of Coronavirus on Households across America*, Sept. 2020.

50. NPR et al., *The Impact of Coronavirus*; Sharon Cohen, "Millions of Hungry Americans Turn to Food Banks for 1st Time," AP News, Dec. 7, 2020.

51. Steffie Woolhandler et al., "Public Policy and Health in the Trump Era," *Lancet* 397, no. 10275 (Feb. 10, 2021).

52. Daniel Funke and Katie Sanders, "Lie of the Year: Coronavirus Downplay and Denial," PolitiFact, Dec. 16, 2020.

Chapter 6

1. "Transcript: Melania Trump's RNC Speech," CNN, Aug. 26, 2020, https://www.cnn.com/2020/08/26/politics/melania-trump-speech-transcript/index.html.

2. David Frost, *"I Gave Them a Sword": Behind the Scenes of the Nixon Interviews* (New York: William Morrow, 1978), 183.

3. 166 Cong. Rec. S650 (daily ed. Jan. 29, 2020); Donald J. Trump, "Remarks by President Trump at Turning Point USA's Teen Student Action Summit 2019" (remarks, Washington, DC, July 23, 2019), White House, https://trumpwhitehouse.archives.gov/briefings-statements /remarks-president-trump-turning-point-usas-teen-student-action-summit-2019/; Miles Taylor, "Former Chief of Staff of Trump's DHS Is the Newest Republican Voter Against Trump," YouTube, Aug. 17, 2020, video, 2:11, https://www.youtube.com/watch?v=OgQZExTciQM&feature =emb_logo.

4. Eric Alterman, *Lying in State: Why Presidents Lie—and Why Trump Is Worse* (New York: Basic Books, 2020), xi.

5. Alterman, *Lying in State*, xi.

6. Pickering v. Bd. of Educ., 391 U.S. 563, 568 (1968).

7. Catherine J. Ross, *Lessons in Censorship: How Schools and Courts Subvert Students' First Amendment Rights* (Cambridge, MA: Harvard University Press, 2015), 87–91, 112–16.

8. *Pickering*, 391 U.S. 563; Connick v. Myers, 461 U.S. 138 (1983); Garcetti v. Ceballos, 547 U.S. 410 (2006).

9. *Garcetti*, 547 U.S. at 426.

10. *Garcetti*, 547 U.S. 410.

11. Adams v. Bd. of Educ. of Harvey Sch. Dist. 152, 968 F.3d 713, 716 (7th Cir. 2020).

12. Alexander S. Vindman, "Alexander Vindman: Coming Forward Ended My Career. I Still Believe Doing What's Right Matters," opinion, *Washington Post*, Aug. 1, 2020.

13. Vindman, "Coming Forward."

14. Rebecca Tan, "Maryland State Employee Fired After Supporting Kenosha Shooting Suspect Kyle Rittenhouse on Facebook," *Washington Post*, Aug. 30, 2020; Pamela Wood, "Maryland Official Fired for Social Media Posts Defending Teen Accused in Kenosha Killings," *Baltimore Sun*, Aug. 29, 2020, https://www.baltimoresun.com/politics/bs-md-pol-mac -love-20200829-grm2qvd5q5g2ppiuzioobylshq-story.html.

15. United States v. Nat'l Treasury Employees Union, 513 U.S. 454, 461–462, 464 (1995) (Stevens, J.).

16. Nixon v. Fitzgerald, 457 U.S. 731 (1982).

17. Wood v. Georgia, 370 U.S. 375, 394–395 (1962).

18. Bond v. Floyd, 385 U.S. 116, 132, 135–136 (1966).

19. Lorelei Laird, "DOJ Says Trump's Tweets Are Official Presidential Statements," *ABA Journal*, Nov. 14, 2017; Trump v. Hawaii, 138 S. Ct. 2392, 2437 n.1 (2018) (Sotomayor, J., dissenting, citing App. 133).

20. Knight First Amendment Inst. at Columbia Univ. v. Trump, 953 F.3d 216, 218–219 (2nd Cir. 2020) (denying en banc review), vacated, No. 20–197 (U.S. Apr. 5, 2021) (ordering dismissal as moot).

21. Notification of Removal, Carroll v. Trump, No. 160694/2019 (N.Y. Sup. Ct. Sept. 8, 2020).

22. Opinion, Carroll v. Trump, No. 20-cv-7311 (S.D.N.Y. Oct. 27, 2020).

23. Alterman, *Lying in State*, xi.

24. United States v. Moore, 612 F.3d 698, 701 (D.C. Cir. 2010) (Ginsburg, J.); Brief for Court-Appointed Amicus Curiae at 39–43, United States v. Flynn, No. 1:17-cr-232 (D.D.C. June 10, 2020).

25. Frank O. Bowman III, *High Crimes and Misdemeanors: A History of Impeachment for the Age of Trump* (Cambridge: Cambridge University Press, 2019), 275–76.

Chapter 7

1. 167 Cong. Rec. S676 (daily ed. Feb. 12, 2021) (statement of Mr. van der Veen); Proceedings of the United States Senate in the Impeachment Trial of Donald John Trump, Part II, S. Doc. No. 117-2, at 150 (2021) (Trial Memorandum of Donald J. Trump, 45th President of the United States of America), https://www.govinfo.gov/content/pkg/CDOC-117sdoc2/pdf /CDOC-117sdoc2-pt2.pdf.

2. Charles L. Black, *Impeachment: A Handbook* (New Haven, CT: Yale University Press, 1998), 37.

3. Michael J. Gerhardt, *The Federal Impeachment Process: A Constitutional and Historical Analysis*, 3rd ed. (Chicago: University of Chicago Press, 2019), 109.

4. Kathryn S. Olmsted and Eric Rauchway, "Richard M. Nixon, 1969–1974," in *Presidential Misconduct: George Washington to Today*, ed. James M. Banner (New York: New Press, 2019), 371.

5. Ralph K. Winter Jr., *Watergate and the Law: Political Campaigns and Presidential Power* (Washington, DC: American Enterprise Institute for Public Policy Research, 1974), 54.

6. Adam Nagourney and Peter Baker, "For Bill Clinton, a Chance to Address a Party That Has Left Him Behind," *N.Y. Times*, updated Sept. 17, 2020.

7. Kathryn Cramer Brownell, "William J. Clinton, 1993–2001," in Banner, *Presidential Misconduct*, 440–46.

8. 145 Cong. Rec. 587–589 (1999) (statement of Rep. Lindsey Graham).

9. Brownell, "William J. Clinton," 440–46.

10. Nixon v. Fitzgerald, 457 U.S. 731, 757–758 (1982).

11. Jared P. Cole and Todd Garvey, *Impeachment and Removal*, CRS Report No. R44260 (Washington, DC: Congressional Research Service, 2015), 7.

12. Benjamin F. Wright, ed., *The Federalist Papers* (New York: MetroBooks, 2002), No. 65, 426, 428.

13. McCulloch v. Maryland, 17 U.S. (1 Wheat.) 316, 407 (1819).

14. Neal Kumar Katyal, "Legislative Constitutional Interpretation," *Duke Law Journal* 50, no. 5 (Mar. 2001): 1382.

15. Nixon v. United States, 506 U.S. 224, 245 (1993).

16. See Richard Primus, "The Limits of Enumeration," *Yale Law Journal* 124, no. 3 (Dec. 2014): 581, 581 n.14.

17. See Stanley Bach and Jack Maskell, *Overview of Electoral College Procedure and the Role of Congress*, CRS Report No. M-111700 (Washington, DC: Congressional Research Service, 2000).

18. Arden Farhi et al., "We Asked All 50 Senators Whether They Agree with Trump That He Won the Election. Only 5 Responded," CBS News, Feb. 19, 2021.

19. Todd Garvey, *The Constitutionality of Censuring the President*, CRS Report No. LSB10096 (Washington, DC: Congressional Research Service, 2018); Jane Hudiberg and Christopher M. Davis, *Resolutions to Censure the President: Procedure and History*, CRS Report No. R45087 (Washington, DC: Congressional Research Service, Feb. 1, 2021).

20. Scott Wong, "Pelosi Rules Out Censure After Trump Acquittal," *The Hill*, Feb. 13, 2021 (referencing censure of former Rep. Charles Rangel).

21. Donald J. Trump (@realDonaldTrump), Twitter, July 30, 2020, 8:46 A.M.

22. Steven G. Calabresi, "Trump Might Try to Postpone the Election. That's Unconstitutional," opinion, *N.Y. Times*, July 30, 2020.

23. Nicholas Fandos, "Deepening Schism, McConnell Says Trump 'Provoked' Capitol Mob," *N.Y. Times*, Jan. 19, 2021.

24. Proceedings of the United States Senate in the Impeachment Trial of Donald John Trump, Part II, S. Doc. No. 117-2, at 146 (2021) (Trial Memorandum of Donald J. Trump, 45th President of the United States of America), https://www.govinfo.gov/content/pkg /CDOC-117sdoc2/pdf/CDOC-117sdoc2-pt2.pdf.

25. "Constitutional Law Scholars on President Trump's First Amendment Defense," Feb. 5, 2021, https://int.nyt.com/data/documenttools/first-amendment-lawyers-trump-impeach ment-defense/7fc3e63ae077f83d/full.pdf.

26. Liz Cheney, "Cheney: I Will Vote to Impeach the President," Congresswoman Liz Cheney, Jan. 12, 2021, https://cheney.house.gov/2021/01/12/cheney-i-will-vote-to-impeach-the -president/.

27. Brandenburg v. Ohio, 395 U.S. 444, 447 (1969).

28. H.R. Res. 24, Cong. 117 (2021).

29. Mary Papenfuss, "GOP Arizona County Chair Slams Twisted Republican Recount as 'Dangerous,'" HuffPost, May 15, 2021.

30. Ipsos, "Reuters/Ipsos: Trump's Coattails (04/02/2021)," press release, Apr. 2, 2021, https://www.ipsos.com/sites/default/files/ct/news/documents/2021-04/topline_write_up _reuters_ipsos_trump_coattails_poll_-_april_02_2021.pdf.

31. "Liz Cheney's Remarks on the House Floor on the Night Before Her Expected Removal from Leadership Post," CNN, May 11, 2021.

32. Jonathan Martin, "Overthrow of a Party Leader Risks Worsening Republicans' Headaches," *N.Y. Times*, May 13, 2021, A18.

33. Adam Barnes, "124 Retired Generals and Admirals Question Biden's Mental Health," *The Hill*, May 12, 2021; "Open Letter from Retired Generals and Admirals," Flag Officers 4 America, May 16, 2021, https://img1.wsimg.com/blobby/go/fb7c7bd8-097d-4e2f-8f12 -3442d151b57d/downloads/2021%20Open%20Letter%20from%20Retired%20Generals%20 and%20Adm.pdf?ver=1621254456411.

34. Peter W. Stevenson, "The 5-Minute Fix," *Washington Post*, May 14, 2021, https://s2 .washingtonpost.com/camp- rw/?trackId=596b84f7ae7e8a44e7d8eeb7&s=609ee9769d2fdae3 024fe9a3&linknum=4&l inktot=40.

35. Sophia Rosenfeld, *Democracy and Truth: A Short History* (Philadelphia: University of Pennsylvania Press, 2019), 173–74.

INDEX

ACKNOWLEDGMENTS

Although I had been writing and thinking about the constitutional status of lies for several years, developments during the Trump presidency shifted the focus of this project. Unfolding events led me to write this book quickly—entirely during the pandemic lockdown—and to revise it even more rapidly between the January 6 insurrection and the second Senate trial of former president Trump. As a result, my primary debt is to all the people who offered unflagging support despite my silence and neglect.

That said, many people contributed to this project.

Walter Biggins, the editor-in-chief at the University of Pennsylvania Press, took on my book as part of his personal editorial portfolio. Mary Francis, director of the press, initially encouraged me to write this book for a general audience. Their enthusiasm and help in framing the project, and Walter's ongoing support and editorial suggestions, were invaluable. The two anonymous readers who read an early version of the manuscript offered valuable comments; I thank them for pushing me in ways that significantly improved this book. Sigal Ben-Porath, whom I first met at the Institute for Advanced Study in Princeton and with whom I have discussed many overlapping interests over the years, got things moving: she piqued the Press's interest in this book before I had figured it out.

Dean Dayna Matthew at George Washington University Law School provided unflagging support and helpful substantive comments. I thank her and the Law School for institutional support. Reference librarian Mary Kate Hunter brought her characteristic eye for detail, problem-solving determination, and enthusiasm to the project. I could not have produced this book so quickly without her help. I also thank Ariella Cassell and Samuel Moore, my indispensable research assistants.

Chapters 2 and 3 draw in part on my previous work: "Ministry of Truth: Why Law Can't Stop Prevarications, Bullshit and Straight-Out Lies in Political Campaigns," *First Amendment Law Review* 16 (2018): 367; and "Incredible

Lies," *University of Colorado L. Rev.* 89 (2018): 377. For helpful comments at workshops and conferences, I thank my colleagues at George Washington University Law School, who generously gave feedback at three internal talks, as well as the faculty at the University of Baltimore Law School, the participants in the Symposium on Fake News and Free Speech held at the University of North Carolina Law School in October 2017, and the Rothberger Conference on Truth, Lies and the Constitution held at the University of Colorado Law School in April 2017.

Several people generously read the entire manuscript. Each of them brought a unique eye and editing style that helped me refine the work. I thank Thomas Remington, Nancy Roth-Remington, and my brother-in-law Eric Rieder for their detailed comments. And a special thanks to Danny Greenberg, whose quid pro quo for reading the manuscript was that I attribute all errors to him, which I gladly do. For professional guidance at several junctures, and decades of friendship, I thank Stuart Klawans. Bali Miller, Nancy Miller, Kenny Roberts, and Claudia Sussman also weighed in at critical junctures.

Many others are part of my valued network of friends and family— fortunately not mutually exclusive categories in my life. I won't name the rest here (you know who you are) but would like them to know how much I appreciated their patience when I could not answer one more email or face one more Zoom get-together. Their presence in my life keeps me going.

With no disrespect to the readers mentioned above, my husband, Jonathan Rieder, is simply the best editor I have ever known. He worked his magic again on this book. As we weathered the pandemic together, he heroically kept everything running so that I could focus almost exclusively on my manuscript, even as he balanced his own teaching and research. More important, we celebrated our fortieth wedding anniversary as I wrapped up the manuscript; that speaks for itself.

My son, Daniel Ross-Rieder, the truth-seeker to whom I dedicated this book, keeps me intellectually challenged and accountable with his insistence on verifiable facts and clear-headed analysis regardless of setting or topic. Daniel and his significant other, Sara Diressova, provide me with loving ballast in a turbulent world.

I could not write this book without thinking about my father, Alexander I. Ross, born Rosovsky. He arrived in the United States in December 1940 as a teenager fleeing the Nazis with his parents and his brother, Henry Rosovsky. They had been essentially stateless since my grandparents fled Russia after the Bolshevik Revolution, gradually moving west through Europe. My father inculcated in me an immigrant's appreciation of US citizenship, democracy, and freedom, including the freedom to speak our minds. The counterpart to that faith is a visceral reaction to authoritarianism and an awareness of the need for constant vigilance. Those values have motivated—and, in turn, been fortified by—my life's work.